Introduction

*A*mazing Stories From New Brunswick" is the sixth in a series of *books produced by Peter D. Clark, dealing with true stories, legends* *places from our Province's past and present.*

Clark's venture into writing began modestly with the idea that he *deal primarily with personal experiences lived in the wilderness of* *'runswick, drawing as well on adventures lived and related by friends* *cquaintances. From there, he has broadened his vistas to include* *wn and country. All along the way, his research into our Province's* *lk re and institutions has been spurred by a double aspiration: to* *serve stories of people and places which with the passing of players* *ld otherwise be lost to future generations and to make these stories* *cessible to present and future readers. Peter Clark is making yet another* *iluable contribution to the cultural heritage of New Brunswick.*

Acknowledgements:

Several individuals have been instrumental in the compiling of this book. Behind the scenes, my lovely wife Sylvie helped out with many facets of the book. Dalton London, once again offered positive support and was a tremendous help as my editor. June Campbell played an active role as my trusted typist. I am deeply indebted to each and every artist for their magnificent contributions.

Special thanks to the following people: Danny and Linda Grant and their family, Blane Little, Vernon Mooers, Royce Van Horne, Bob McAllister, Wayne Phillips, Anne Reynolds, Tim Gillies, Jack Van Wart, Arnie Wilkins, Ernie and Winona McLean, Leroy Tucker, Fred H. Harris, Frank C. MacDonald, Kathryn Meyer, Paul Janssens, Bill Thorpe, Tom Scovill, Frank Shute, Burton S. Moore, Howard and Muriel Moore, as well as The New Brunswick Sports Hall of Fame, *The Daily Gleaner* (Bruce Hallihan and Bill Hunt) and *The Northside News*. I'd personally like to thank the many individuals whom I interviewed for information. I'd also like to thank my friends and family for their encouragement and anyone that I may have forgotten.

– Peter D. Clark

DEDICATION
TO
DANNY GRANT

CONTENTS:

School Life in the 50's and 60's   1

Ernie McLean (The Only Canadian Stock Car Promoter   12
   named to Canadian Motor Sports Hall of Fame)

An Otter Named George   20

Lumber Camp Stories and More as told by   23
   Frank C. MacDonald 1890 - 1981

The Paris Crew of Saint John   29

A Taste of Tart's   38

Winter Horse Races at Gagetown   40

Memories from Frank Shute   43

Golden Memories of my Canadian Literacy and   47
   Book Tour, February - October 1999

The Tobique, Then and Now   63

The Danny Grant Story   67

ILLUSTRATORS:

Nick Gallagher   6, 9, 25, 28, 39

Russell London   21, 27, 41

*Front Cover Painting by **BRUNO BOBAK***
*Title: **Slate Island on the Miramichi***

Bruno Bobak

Bruno Bobak was born in Wawelowka, Poland and has resided in Fredericton since 1960. Bruno began his impressive art career as a Canadian war artist during World War II. His career flourished and today he is internationally recognized and his paintings are in evidence around the world in public and private collections.

In 1995 the distinguished title of "Order of Canada" was bestowed upon Bruno for his contributions to the art community in Canada.

School Life in the 50's and 60's

I started my schooling at Albert Street School in 1955 at the age of 5. My birthday was December 26 so they allowed me to start early. I am also certain that with 6 children in the family, one more child out the door from our 628 Chestnut Street household was a welcome relief for my mother, Dorothy.

Suffice it to say that as a rule, we towed the line. If you acted up in school and the teacher called home, you would get a good spanking. If you were a nuisance in class you might have lines to write out, receive a couple of whacks from the yard stick, a pointer across the knuckles or the strap. For the most part children were brought up in disciplined homes.

My first experience with a girlfriend was in grade one. How could you forget that? Her name was Barb Thibodeau. We used to walk hand and hand. Older kids would encourage us to smooch or smack the lips and of course we would oblige. We were quite shy and innocent that's for sure.

I remember that all through elementary that each class would have posters with the children's names. As a reward system gold stars were issued for work in subjects such as spelling, arithmetic, language arts, etc.

Most teachers had little tricks in helping students memorize. A big word like Arithmetic was relatively easy to learn. (A Rat In Tom's House Might Eat Tom's Ice-Cream.) It seemed that we were continuously memorizing things like "Flander's Field", "The Lord is My Shepherd", etc.

I was the "teacher's pet" in one of my elementary classes. The teacher, who shall remain anonymous, had a habit of piercing my ear-lobes with her long fingernails. I eventually got infection, visited the doctor and came to school with a note from home telling her what had happened.

Vernon Mooers went to Devon School for grades one and two, then attended the new South Devon School in the mid-fifties from grades 3-6. Here are some of his recollections:

"The music program wasn't instrument training but just consisted of choral singing and I was a "crow". Other groups of students had various songbird names. The "crows" were supposed to lipsync, but in the Annual Music Festival Competition held at George Street High School - I just couldn't hold back and sang out - which is probably why we lost!

South Devon School was new and when school administrator, Nellie Winters, came to visit we all cringed. I also remember we had a class draw to exchange Christmas presents and Fred McElman got my name. We were friends, having done some science experiments in his basement. His gift to me was a hockey stick he bought at Lean's grocery on Main Street and was expensive. What a surprise! I was elated. Fred went on to become a lawyer and got the distinguished "Order of Canada" in 2002.

I remember 'Hot Dog' Hossack won the math prize for the school. Today he drives cab; Brent Bishop, on the other hand, was a kid always in hot water with the teachers. When he got a little older he was sentenced to the Youth Training School for petty crimes at Kingsclear. When he got out he went by the straight and narrow and went on to become a successful real estate tycoon. So you never know."

Sometimes we used to get embarrassed by a teacher. One time I wrote a story about Brucey Murray, my best friend, at the time. Well I misspelled Brucey and she read the story to the class pronouncing the name as I had spelled it. I wrote 'Brushy did this' and 'Brushy did that' and of course the class cracked up laughing. I was a little more careful with my spelling after that.

I remember in grade 3 falling off the slide and breaking my collarbone. Jim Huey, who was in grade 7, carried me home. He later became an ambulance driver here in Fredericton. It was Dr. Stickles who came to the house and fixed me up. It's too bad doctors who make house calls are ancient history.

2

I remember one time in grade 8, Larry Schleyer and I pulled a bit of a prank on Eddie Smith. He lived down near Roy's Pool Hall on King Street and often went there for lunch. He was always tardy.

Well, one day we taped 2 tacks to the seat and 2 to the back of his chair. He came into class, late as usual, pulled out his chair and slumped into the chair. Hello for screaming. You could have heard the yell from one side of the school to the other. The teacher inquired as to who were the guilty culprits and of course Larry and I fessed up. He took us in the next room and administered corporal punishment, the strap five times on each hand to Larry first. When it came to my turn he let me off with detention detail. I was too small.

Bob McAllister taught school from 1961 - 1990. He said that for the most part the students were pretty good in the 60's. Sometimes in class if the noise got a little loud he would turn the lights down low. He remembers a boy named Jim Wilson as getting the strap regularly once a week. The kids used to bring water pistols to school in the spring. One particular incident stands out.

"I used to have a bookcase with a mirror that the kids couldn't see. I could write on the board and keep an eye on the class. One day this black student Tyrone McIntyre from the Doak Road was shooting off his squirt gun while I was working at the board. Little did he know that I caught him red- handed thanks to the mirror. I walked over to him just as he was putting it in his desk. I jammed the desk down and said that I was breaking it on him. I'll never forget what he said in a thick accent,

'You'll neva break that sur, it's rubbah'

I had one student named Bucky Murray 3 years in a row. I finally suggested that he join the navy and he did."

Probably one of Bob's most illustrious students was Matt Stairs.

At the end of the school year all ink was confiscated. At that time all the students used fountain pens and the principal was afraid some of the bottles would be thrown at the school. In the early 60's there were no buses to school. We either walked, biked or our parents drove us to school. One student around 1968 drove a Lincoln Continental to school. He was 16 and his name was Chip Vale.

Guelda McCarty taught the opportunity class in the 1960's. This was a small class and the students were there for numerous reasons. If they were dyslexic, mentally challenged, slow learners, children who didn't fit in the mainstream, she got them. My brother Jim was there. He hated school and missed a lot due to illness. Guelda gave the kids a lot of attention and tried to make them feel special. She even washed clothes for the children. Many of the students went on to have successful careers.

Ruth McGirr taught the accelerated class at Albert Street School. This was a special class of gifted students from the school district who completed 3 grades in 2 years. She taught grade 7 and part of 8. The class consisted of the brightest students who were recommended by grade 6 teachers. Not all students who were nominated attended. She remembers the students as being well-adjusted and experienced very few problems concerning discipline. There was plenty of work and the kids that were caught up were always busy with other school projects.

I remember what happened one day in grade 10, in Mrs. Delong's class. This pair of sneakers and gym shorts were thrown across the room by Bill M. Of course he threw them when she wasn't looking and they hit me in the head. I just fired them back across the room. She asked who did it and of course I owned up. I was sent down to visit Raymond Woodworth, the principal, who gave me the strap.

One other time we had a supply teacher. The biggest guy in the class, Bobby Dymond, dared me to light a wooden sulphur match. Of course I did, not knowing that the sulphur smell would be so strong. The teacher asked who lit the match and of course I raised my hand. He made me clean all of the gum off the desks with a knife which was no easy task.

In my first year in grade 10 I got expelled for not doing my work. I was allowed back in but failed miserably. In my second year I got expelled again for insubordination, refusing to get my hair cut because it was over my ears. At the time guys like Tommy Blizzard, Nick Hamilton and Jack Van Wart were exempt because they played in a band. I went downtown and inquired about going into the army. However, I decided to give school another try and I opted to go before the superintendent Murray Sargeant who was a strict but fair man. He drew up a contract for me to abide by the rules and to make a 70% average. I passed the year but went out West the following year.

In my second year of grade 10 Ted Weyman and I figured we had a score to settle. The arrangement was to meet down on the green. Of course everyone in school knew and around one hundred spectators showed up. After the fight we shook hands and had a greater respect for each other. That's the way things were settled, one on one.

Anne Reynolds told me that she remembers walking down the middle of the road to school in the middle of a snowstorm. Schools were seldom cancelled. The girls, Jane Hilborn and Ann Wilson also were wearing skirts. You see they were not allowed slacks back then. One girl actually got frostbite. Her name was Jill Spicer. Another girl, Susan Rouse, made national news at the time for defying the rules and wearing slacks. The year was 1970. She was not allowed in class and spent the days in Mr. Woodworth's office. Eventually her father, Doug pulled her out of school. The next year, 1971, her father became a school board member. Many of the members advocated that the policy of dresses or skirts only was to be rescinded.

In high school, I think a lot of the kids tried smoking at one time or another. At lunch time many of the male persuasion would head to the Cue 88 Pool Hall on Regent Street for a game of 8-ball or snooker. The girls had their own place, The Susie-Cue, a couple of doors down. The Cue-88 could be a rough place on a Friday or Saturday night.

In high school if you didn't graduate in three years, you were on something called the plan. It took me five years but I dun graduated. One of my friends, Jack Van Wart was on the plan - six years to graduate. He said that in each grade he got the facts and the second year he started to gather them all in and digest them. He said that by the time he graduated he was pretty good on his ga zintas, you know 2 goes inta 8 4 times and his cypherin was exceptional. He also played in the band on a regular basis and was making a little cash. One day he fell

asleep in class and got rudely awakened when a 5 pound Modern World History book came crashing onto his noggin'. I don't know if the teacher knocked any sense into him but he sure work up in a hurry. He also never fell asleep in that class again.

After a year out of school in 1968 I wasn't any better prepared for first term. I was a regular detainee for not having my work done. Finally after scraping by first term I started to smarten up. Mrs. Unger, our Math teacher, was one of the finest that I had in high school. She used to make sure that we knew our algebra and geometry which was graded out of 200. Anyone who didn't grasp the concepts was strongly encouraged to stay for extra help. I made 152 on Math and kept my marks up in grade 11.

It was Derek Brown who convinced me to try rugby as a sport in grade ll. Bill Thorpe was the head coach and we had A and B teams. When I first started practices I was a smoker. Bill ran extremely hard workouts. Our warm-up was a mile run followed by stretching and callisthenics. My lungs were burning up from the workouts and I threw away the cigarettes. I managed to make the A team after a couple of games. The highlight of the fall season was something called "The Fall Frolic Days". We would play a rugby game on the Friday afternoon and 1500 screaming F.H.S. fans would cheer us on. In 1970 the event was held at College Field and we defeated our arch enemies, Saint John High. If it wasn't for the sport of rugby I probably wouldn't have graduated.

I met up with an old schoolmate Arnie Wilkins recently. He told me that he too had a rough time at high school. At the beginning of one year he was sent down to the office and told to "shape up or ship out". The principal wasn't going to put up with any of his stunts this year. He politely asked one of his teachers if she minded if he sat at the front of the class. It might help him to pay attention. She said, "You are better off at the back. I don't want to have your face in front of me as a constant reminder that I have to have you in my class for a second year."

In grade 12 Mrs. B. was a saint to put up with our class. I remember her famous quote about me. I was taking 4 subjects. "Time will pass, but will you, because Mr. Clark obviously will not." I remember one day she asked a question to Tom Blizzard. He didn't have the foggiest notion of what she asked as he was daydreaming. He answered, "Hot dogs, hamburgs, get 'em while they last" and well you can imagine the mayhem and bedlam in the class.

I remember talking with a guidance counsellor about my options after getting out of high school. She stated to consider a trade school or go directly into the work-force but university would not be an option. Well those were just the words I needed. I graduated on four subjects, 51.8 but I made higher on my provincial matriculation papers and got accepted at St. Thomas University where I eventually graduated with two degrees. You never know what you can do in life. One of my English teachers in high school would roll over in her grave if she knew I had written 6 books.

Nick Gallagher

Nick Gallagher was born in Fredericton, N.B. in 1976. He is currently enrolled at Saint Thomas University, B.Ed. program. Nick specializes in cartooning. In 1994 Nick illustrated the book of short stories "Woods, Streams, Ghosts and Hangin's".

Ernie McLean
(The Only Canadian Stock Car Promotor named to Canadian Motor Sports Hall of Fame)

Ernest Edward McLean was born April 25, 1936 at the County's Poor House in Chatham, N.B. and was raised by his great uncle George in Barnaby River, 25 miles southwest of Chatham. He attended a one-room school house in Semiwagon Ridge finishing grade 8 at age 14. At the age of 15 Ernie began working in the woods. He remembers, "When I was a young fellah I cut 5 cord of pulp with a buck saw. I got the wood off crown land and sold it for $28.00. I bought a train ticket to Moncton and eventually found my mother's home at River Glade, about twenty miles southwest of Moncton."

"When I first came to River Glade in 1950 I pumped gas for Bernard Nelson at the Irving station. I worked in Moncton, working in garages for $35.00 a week. Our week was 6 days with Sundays off. Some of the places I worked were Job O'Brien's, Les Jones and Alex E. Ross's as a mechanic. Eventually I became a licensed mechanic."

Ernie married a New Brunswick girl (Winona) in December 1954 and had four children: Angela, Teresa, Gary and William.

Eventually Winona and Ernie moved to Ontario to seek their fame and fortune. In 1957 he had met the now legendary Jim Hallihan who introduced him to car racing. In 1958 he became a licensed mechanic in the province of Ontario and leased a Fina Service station. They began to visit the Pine Crest Speedway. In 1959 Jim sold Ernie a jalopy stock car and Ernie got the bug. He raced at places like Pine Crest, Flamboro, Nilestown, Sutton and CNE. At that time winners were taking home 20 or 25 bucks. At Pine Crest the place was jam-packed. At night you would be lucky to get in the main event. Ernie always managed to get in, never winning but always in the thick of things.

Left to right: Dave Fawcett, Ernie MacLean, Ralph Trites

By 1964 the family decided to come back to New Brunswick. Ernie had scouted out some businesses but couldn't settle on anything that really suited him. He decided to move back to River Glade, NB. For some time now, he had it in his mind to build a stock car track. He came down at Easter time, discussed his vision with a number of people and the consensus was that the stock car races would pass with flying colours. Ernie and Winona purchased an old farm in River Glade from Bessie Goggin. The family moved down the long weekend in May and soon Ernie had a job at Drury's Transport in Petitcodiac.

He worked his day job and in his spare time he carved out a quarter mile dirt track oval. By August the track was open for business.

One of his major obstacles was the financing. He had visited a number of banks earlier on. They turned him down saying he didn't have a job and there are no stock cars racing in this area. Hovever, he did have enough money saved for a down payment on the farm. He remembered the first mortgage he got was 13% which was very high at that time. He approached anyone he knew that might be able to help him. After he got going and had the track paved the banks were more than willing to lend him the money. He said he had to wheel and deal, scrounge like a pack-rat, whatever he had to do to get off the ground. It just goes to show that if you set your mind to something, believe in yourself, anything is possible.

River Glade Speedway

The year after River Glade opened the place was packing them in. You couldn't walk between the grand-stand and the race-track. Additional revenues came in from programs, souvenirs and the canteen. But if it wasn't for Winona and the kids, Ernie admits, he could never have succeeded.

One day he had the kids pick up the garbage from the evening before. When the kids finished they came over proud as punch. Ernie asked what he owed them. They all looked to Billy, the youngest but the smartest when it came to money. He spoke up, "Whatever you would pay someone else." Anyway I knew they would have to be rewarded.

"We were averaging anywhere from 1, 3, to 4 thousand people a night. We would be disappointed if we didn't get 3000. We used to have as many as 80 cars in the races. The same people that I had begged and pleaded for money now bent over backwards to provide financing. One of the banks was the Bank of Commerce in Salisbury as well as numerous individuals. We were over the danger point at that stage of the game. There was enough money coming in to pay the bills and get ahead a bit."

The racing caught on so well that in 1965 Ernie took on a partner, Jerry Campbell, and River Glade Speedway became the first asphalt oval for stock car racing in the Maritimes. Grandstands, announcers, tower, canteens and washrooms were built.

Racing was also better organized with a good set of rules. For instance the cars had to be equipped with a roll cage and all cars had to have full bodies. If a fender came off then it had to be replaced. The cars had to have fire extinguishers. It was always a battle enforcing the rules. There was always some guy who said he never had to do that before. There had to be lap belts and proper shoulder harnesses. Either the drivers had them installed or they didn't race.

Giving the sport a little extra profile, Ernie introduced the "extra distance" event to the Maritimes, with the inaugural "International" as their "first big win." Guys like Earl Ross, Don Beiderman and Jr. Hanley, Frank Fraser, Caleb Dunn, Paul Lewis as well as New England drivers Ralph Nason and Russ Nutting, to name a few, were frequent racers at the track.

Cars came from all over: Saint John, Miramichi, Campbellton, Fredericton, Nova Scotia and the States. The payout was pretty good but not enough to make any one rich. It was a sport with sponsors' names on the cars. Someone might donate tires or gas or something. If a person was lucky and won the main event he might go home with 150 dollars. Occasionally throughout the year there might be a major event that would pay 1000 dollars. Another aspect of promotion was a point fund and at the end of the year trophies or cash money were handed out. Every race counted throughout the year. People participated in the sport for the love of the sport just like golfing. It was something that got in your blood.

As years went on the sport of stock car racing grew in leaps and bounds. Many new tracks opened up around New Brunswick. Some of the operators were just in it for a quick buck and of course they didn't last long. "They figured we were just coining it," Ernie explained. Ernie actually leased some of the financially troubled tracks because it was to his advantage. There were cars coming out of those areas racing at the River Glade track. Some of the new ones at the time were; The Miramichi Speedway, Fredericton's Brookside Speedway, Danny's Speedbowl at Bathurst, McEwan at Moncton, Havre Boucher, N.S. and at Antigonish, N.S..

"At one time I operated River Glade on Saturday and Havre Boucher near the causeway in N.S. on Sunday. I called the drive down, 'Running the Old Sunrise Trail' because it was a rugged job travelling to and fro and getting ready for the races. We loved what we were doing at the time and making some money was an added bonus. Even though the season was short, May to September, there was plenty to do in the off season. My principal vocation was chasing down sponsorships for the following season.

I remember a story about my early days at the track. I had no money and was just scraping by, by the skin of my teeth. I was working for Drury's Transport in Petitcodiac. As it was getting closer to the opening of the season at my track I was taking more time off. Gosh they got lucky if I got 2 full days in a week. Les Drury, my boss, called me into his office and said, 'This race track seems to be more important than your job.' I replied, 'It really is because I will make more in one race than I will here in one year.' He said, 'Well if that is the case, you better go home and tend to it.' I still don't know if he fired me or just let me go. It didn't bother me because I was close to getting the track open. We had a lot of fun at the track over the years."

In the early 1970's to draw more people in, Ernie the Promotor brought from New England the Super Modifieds (NESMRA) under the management of Ken Smith and Russ Conway. The quick fuel injected machines appeared at River Glade each year and thereafter at other regional tracks as well.

Ernie had an abundance of energy, experience and lots of ideas. Places like the Miramichi Speedway and Fredericton's Brookside stayed afloat because of him.

Ernie introduced the 4 cylinder mini stocks and 6 cylinder chargers to the line up. This appealed to both fans and to the new drivers who began to take up the sport.

Ernie was instrumental in forming the touring series, MASCAR, and even allowed the series to capitalize on his "Name Race" by making the Canada Day 100, Eastern 75 and the now famous "International" to become part of the MASCAR Schedule. Always willing to adapt, Ernie did what it took to make racing popular on the Maritime front. He paid the largest late model purse to MASCAR topping the scales at $15,000, an unbelievable amount in the 80's.

Ernie tells of bringing the late and great Dale Earnhardt in:

"I was looking to bring a driver in. Bobby Allison had won the Daytona 500 that year and I thought he would be a suitable candidate. We signed him up but he had a bad accident at Pocono and was forced to cancel. The agent called me up and asked if I would accept Dale Earnhardt. He was a pretty big star so it didn't take me long to agree. In those days Dale was a little rough and controversial but was a super guy. We were tickled pink and many of the fans couldn't believe he was coming to River Glade. I had to pay him $10,000 U.S. as soon as his plane touched down in Moncton, regardless of whether the weather was rain, sleet, hail or sunshine. The worst happened. It did rain but we got most of the race in.

Dale Earnhardt

Dale started at the back of the pack of 24 cars. It was a 100 lap race. At the 20th lap, he was halfway up the pack. He was driving my car. The race was called early but I would put money on it that he would have finished first. That was the highlight of my career. I was going to bring him back the next year but General Motors wouldn't allow it because of his commitment to them. Dale was killed at Daytona when he hit the wall in February 2001. I also brought in Alan Kulwicki who later won the Winston Cup Championship. Allen was killed in a plane crash."

Not everything was rosy at the track. The worst horror night that Ernie can remember was when Debbie Hallihan died while racing at Riverside Speedway in Antigonish, Nova Scotia. She lost control on coming into number 2 turn, hit the wall and her seatbelts broke. "Around midnight we heard the worst. She was like a daughter to us," Ernie recalls.

Sometimes drivers had to be disqualified and handed out suspensions. If the drivers organized meetings against River Glade, action had to be taken. One night the drivers decided to go on strike in the middle of the race. Ernie had to call and issue a stern warning to either race or never show their face at this track again. It was a big gamble but most of the men did race. Ernie was a fair man and kept his word. For the few that didn't race he never allowed them back. He gained a great deal of respect from his peers after that evening.

Leroy Tucker was one of the many drivers who knew Ernie on a personal level.

"Ernie was one of the nicest guys in the world. If you did something wrong he had a certain way of telling you without upsetting you. He was the best promotor around - bar none. If you damaged your car he'd call you up to see how you were making out. He would go out of his way to make sure you could get back racing next week. One funny thing Ernie used to say, 'You fellahs are the nicest guys in the world, but when you get in your race car and strap your helmets on, for some of you, your brains go to your feet.' "

Ernie has helped many over the years. He has employed many, some of whom went on to university. He sponsored local sports teams. Thousands of race fans have been thrilled and nurtured in the sport of stock car racing. Many racing drivers have taken home "the green". Corporate sponsors and businesses have benefited financially. If there is a father-figure in the stock car racing, let's call him Ernie McLean.

So it is fitting that Ernest E. McLean should be remembered for being inducted into the Canadian Motor Sport Hall of Fame, February 24, 2001 at Harbour Castle Hotel in Toronto. Hats off to Ernie for a job well done.

Ernie McLean

An Otter Named George

told by Fred H. Harris

While in New Brunswick on a deer-hunting trip I became acquainted with and formed a great liking for a pet of a new kind to me.

The first morning after my arrival I went over to the cook cabin for breakfast.

"Have you seen George this morning?" one of the guides asked the cook.

I couldn't imagine who George was, for I knew all the guides from past trips to the same camp, but as we were sitting down to griddlecakes and coffee, there came a scratching at the back door. When it was opened a sleek black animal, four feet long, ambled in, evidently glad to see us. It was a beautiful tame otter, weighing around 30 lbs.

"Come here, George," said a guide, and held out a griddlecake. The otter took it, and soon he was poking his head into my lap, begging for more. Never have I seen so remarkable and engaging a tame creature of the wild.

Jack, who'd often been my guide, had caught him in the river with his hand, soon after birth, and taken him home. Never confined, sometimes he was away for a week or so, but always returned. When you went outside in a canoe he would swim alongside for perhaps a mile. If you paddled too fast, George would go underwater where he could make better speed.

One summer a sportswoman was playing a trout when George neatly took it from her hook. Later when she had boated a large fish, George

slipped over the side of the canoe, seized her catch, and was gone before she knew it.

George was a good fisherman. Often he would dive and come up with two small trout, one in each side of his mouth. His specialty was eels. When he caught one he would play with it as a cat plays with a mouse, letting it go just for the fun of catching it again.

He loved to have his belly scratched and enjoyed playing rough. The more you rolled him over, the better he liked it. I became very fond of that otter and hoped that he would avoid being trapped.

• •

A couple of falls later, a guide, Arthur Moore, found George the otter crushed between two logs.

Russell London

Russell London was born in Bathurst, N.B. in 1944. He has been a professional artist for 9 years. He was co-winner of the 1995 River Currents Juried Competition. His work is mainly involved with realism.

Lumber Camp Stories and More

as told by Frank C. MacDonald

1890 - 1981

Frank C. MacDonald was born in Deeside, Quebec. He spent his early years working in lumber camps, hunting, trapping and guiding in the woods and on the waters around Campbellton, N.B.. The following excerpts are taken from a manuscript entitled "The Wayward One", which includes some astute memories of that era.

Another important fact about Frank is that he served in the Canadian army during World War I. Private MacDonald's story of being imprisoned and his attempts at escaping are well documented in his book "A Kaiser's Guest" written in 1918.

Frank C. MacDonald

I spent my first full winter in a lumber camp on the Kedgewick River and got a full man's wages, one dollar a day, food and bed. The day was between daylight and dark, summer or winter. The food was the same every day - pork and beans for breakfast, sometimes hot biscuits or flapjacks with black molasses and black tea that turned green when we put the coarse brown sugar in it.

We had two lunches, one in the morning and in the afternoon about three. For our lunch we carried out in a sack or box white bread and brown raisin bread, a pail of salt pork without a trace of lean, a can of molasses and a pail for tea.

Supper was always a beef or pork stew with potatoes and other vegetables, black tea and donuts or cake. On the table for all meals were bowls of prunes and stewed dried apples. Pork and beans were the most important food and a cook who couldn't cook them well did not last long.

The beds were called ramp pastures. They were double deck and ran undivided the full length of the bunk house. The blankets were sewn together and as many as thirty men often slept under one blanket. A night under a blanket with thirty men whose chief food was pork and beans was a memorable experience. The toilets were under God's unbroken roof. Your backside hung over a frozen rail on the edge of a long narrow pit. Toilet paper hadn't been invented yet.

One of the biggest and hardiest races of men in the world grew up in these camps. The men stayed on the job until it was finished. Any lumberjack who left before the finish except for accident, sickness or trouble at home, was soon blacklisted and no one would hire him.

Each camp had a huge chest called the Wanagan Box in which a stock of ointments and linaments for men and horses was kept along with heavy winter clothing which was sold to the men.

The men were divided into small crews and the crew that cut and skidded the most logs got a monthly prize of a pound of tobacco.

No whiskey was ever allowed in the camps, no cards or games of any kind except checkers or dominoes. That was to prevent quarrels. A fight in camp was rare indeed and the fighters were generally dismissed and sometimes blackballed if the fight became known. Consequently, the men kept all their enmities bottled up until the drive came in and they had a few

A ramp pasture

drinks. They fought out all the forgotten quarrels of the long winter. The streets of Campbellton, N.B. saw some famous battles that are not recorded in history.

When the men hit town most of the stores closed up for a couple of days, some boarded up their windows for fear that an overloaded lumberjack would fall through it, as most of the celebrators would gather where there was a light on. Most of street lights were turned off. On a dark night, when a hundred men with steel corked boots tramped around on three paved blocks of Campbellton's Main Street, it looked like a million fireflies had fallen out of the sky.

****

A Cougar Story

I had been shooting partridge with my 30-30 rifle and had only two shells left. When I got back to my camp, I thought the visitor I heard was a bear, took my rifle and crawled out. There was no sound and I could see nothing in the dark. I gave a shout knowing that, if it was a bear, it would run. Nothing moved. I was puzzled but just when I entered my shelter, a heavy animal landed on the roof and gave out a blood curdling scream that I knew well. It was a cougar and I was in a bad spot. I didn't dare to go out, even if I had more ammunition lest he jump off the roof on me. I kept my fire going and sat tight. He moved stealthily about on the roof walking, by the sound, always on the edge. The tarpaper rattled and I finally thought I had located him. I risked firing one of my shells but missed. It sounded as though he jumped across the roof but he didn't leave.

About midnight, he started to tear the roof off. I could hear him tearing up the tarpaper. The split poles that made the roof were not nailed or fastened and he scratched at them and sometimes moved one a little, but it seemed he was standing on them at the same time he was trying to tear them up. About daylight he gave another scream and I heard him jump off the roof. All sounds ceased. When daylight came I cautiously crawled out. He was gone but his big tracks were all over the place, and when I headed back up the stream to the halfway camp, I found his track. He had stalked me for two miles down the trap line the night before.

****

Canadian black bears are not generally dangerous, the exceptions being a bear with cubs. She will attack anything that molests or even approaches her cubs. Any big bear that comes out of his den in the spring, thin and hungry and can't find food is also a dangerous animal. Then, again in the fall of the year when the berry crop that the bears fatten on for their hibernation fails. If he is poor and hungry when it is time to den up, he will attack anything for the black bear is not a coward, although many think he is. Under ordinary circumstances he avoids humans because he has the good sense to stay away from trouble, but he is not a nice fellow to be in a cabin with.

A man who sleeps much in the open will awaken to a very small sound. I awoke in the night to hear the door swing shut. It was moonlight and I could see very well a big lean black bear shut inside the cabin with me. My axe was alongside me in the bunk. I had shot a partridge with my last shell. The empty rifle, packsack and partridge were on the floor. The bear hadn't seen me and never did. He smelled the rifle and the pack, found the partridge and ate it, bones, feathers and all, then he started smelling around the door and the window looking for a way out. He would have succeeded in time, going through whichever way he chose but I was afraid he would discover me first. I reached quietly for my axe and hit the empty drum a blow that sounded in that little cabin like an earthquake. The bear went through the window as if he had been shot out of a cannon and was gone.

The Paris Crew of Saint John

by Paul Janssens

Paul Janssens was former Announcer/Producer at CBC Halifax and Fredericton, former Sports Editor of the Fredericton Daily Gleaner. He is currently practising law in Fredericton.

One hundred years ago a team of tough lumbermen from Saint John, New Brunswick, won a world rowing championship on the Seine in Paris.

Twice they drew well ahead of eight competitors, first in an outrigger shell called *James A. Harding*, and later in a boat rowed from the gunwales.

The muscular gentlemen of the rowing world were incredulous. Who had ever heard of winners from Saint John? And the Paris Crew - as the Saint John team was nicknamed - was challenged first by the States and then by the Èlite of British rowers.

The struggle to prove, then prove again, that the Paris Crew were the champions lasted for four years and culminated in the most exciting, dramatic, and tragic race on the Kennebecasis River on August 23, 1871, when the Tyne team of Britain were defeated.

But the success of the Paris Crew gradually withered. Saint John began to suffer economic difficulties, then the population changed, people moved away, and rowing, as a sport, went out of fashion. Even the story of the Paris Crew's success faded from people's memories and would no doubt have been relegated to the archives had not the Paris Crew been named to

The Paris Crew
Courtesy of New Brunswick Sports Hall of Fame

Canada's Sports Hall of Fame on June 16, 1956. Since then, there has been a renewed interest in the champions of Saint John.

Rowing and sculling were popular sports in Saint John in the mid-1800s. The best oarsmen came from West Saint John or Carleton (whichever one preferred to call it), for there the lads lived by the waterfront and spent most of their time in boats. It was not unusual for a group to get together and buy a "shell". One of these groups was later the famous Paris Crew, and consisted of Robert Fulton, Elijah Ross, Samuel Hutton and James Price.

They began in a small way, by challenging the Indiantown Raftsmen's Association crew in 1863. The poor raftsmen were so outdistanced that they couldn't walk along the street for a while afterwards without having small boys poke fun at them.

The Paris Crew (then known as the Carleton crew) cleaned up again in the summer of 1864. They started the summer of 1865 by showing a stern to seven other New Brunswick crews at Father Duffy's picnic at Sand Cove, and went on to polish off other contenders. In 1866, they rowed four races - and won four. People now began to take notice.

Then in 1867 - the year of Confederation - a tremendous regatta was being held at Paris, with oarsmen participating from most of the principal countries of the world.

The people of Saint John figured the city should be on the sports map and that Robert Fulton, Elijah Ross, George Price, Samuel Hutton and James Price were just the ones to bring fame to the old seaport city. So they passed around the hat and raised $7,000 to send them to France. The rest went into the record books.

The four-man Carleton crew (James Price didn't row but was the reserve oarsman) proved it was not only the fastest crew in New Brunswick, but the fastest anywhere.

There was a bang-up celebration when the quintet came home loaded down with ribbons and silver mugs. The only sour note was injected by United States newspapers which said grudgingly that while the Saint John crew had done fairly well at Paris, they hadn't met the Republican crew of Springfield, Mass.. The newspapers claimed that the Republicans, who hadn't been at Paris, could beat the Carleton crew, which by now was designated the Paris Crew.

Saint John sent a challenge to the Republicans, inviting them to come to New Brunswick and race. The Republicans declined. So, in an effort to prove they were world champions the Paris Crew went to Springfield. The Republicans didn't fare very well and the result was a magnificent victory for the Canadians.

An indication that rowing was big business came when a big-time gambler offered Elijah Ross $10,000 if he'd let the Republicans cross the finish line in first place. The valiant oarsman planted a hamlike fist in the gambler's eye, followed with an uppercut to the jaw, and left him flat on the floor.

Meanwhile, the English, who considered that they had more or less a monopoly on rowing, were vowing to regain the world rowing crown. It didn't make them happy to read such statements as this one from the *Boston Daily Advertiser*:

The four lumbermen from Saint John beat the very flower of English amateurs, the well-known London rowing club, composed from old Varsity oars, the picked four of the Oxford eight which had but lately beaten Cambridge in the great annual university struggle on the Thames.

In 1870 they accepted the challenge of the Tyne crew, of which James Renforth was stroke, for a race at Lachine, Quebec. During this race a heavy squall developed and the boat of the Saint John crew became waterlogged and almost unmanageable.

The English crew had prepared for rough weather by carrying washboards and won the race. They had handed the Paris Crew its first defeat. Saint John's oarsmen granted that the Tyne Crew had gained a fair victory, and offered no excuses but they did request a return race. The result was the challenge for the race on Kennebecasis, arranged for August 23, 1871.

That day must have been one of the most thrilling Saint John ever had. Age-yellowed newspaper files tell us that the residents, old and young alike, were crawling out of bed at three o'clock in the morning.

The city was crowded with sport fans from England, the United States and various parts of Canada - a sight seldom seen since, except for major prize fights, and even that phase of sport has diminished in the port city.

All Saint John, it seemed, was alive to the excitement of the contest. Special trains for East Riverside, the starting line, began leaving Saint John at 4 a.m. and at 5 a.m. as the dark of the early morning gave way to the rising sun, the banks of the Kennebecasis became packed with the gathering masses of people. Old men, young men, boys, girls, young women and old women, all were there to see the great event that was soon to begin.

A newspaper of the day gave this account of the scene:

All about the fields small parties had gathered with packed lunch baskets. Many took the opportunity to stretch out under the trees and catch up on the sleep that had been disturbed by the excitement.

Old women, keen to the commercial possibilities of the occasion, sold apples and ginger bread from stands they had erected along the railroad fence. The grandstands and other erections were alive with the bright colours of ladies' dresses.

Row boats plied on the river, sail boats passed up and down, fleets of woodboats at anchor kept their sails up and their flags flying, while yachts skimmed like birds over the glassy surface of the great river upon which the sculling championship race was to be held. The river was alive with the constant motion of craft of all kinds, and in between them with careless gaiety, dozens of venturesome boys paddled about on make-shift rafts.

From the capital city of Fredericton, the steamship Fawn came with hundreds of spectators and anchored in the stream, while white tug boats, steamers and woodboats constantly arrived and took up positions in the line. The decks of everything that would float were lined with the happy sightseers, and on the various steamers the music from a dozen different bands drifted across the water.

With so much time remaining before the race was to begin at 7:30 a.m., the weather became the main topic of conversation and when a light breeze began to ripple the waters there were anxious looks upon the faces of the gathered thousands. They well knew that rough water would cancel the race, spoiling their sport and thrills. Thus betting on the weather became as brisk as betting on the race. All they talked about was the weather until suddenly in the midst of the doubting, there came a joyous shout: "Here they come!"

All was forgotten and everybody suddenly came to life.

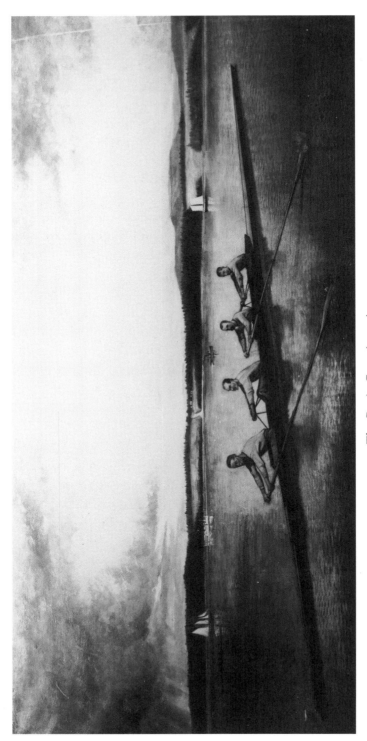

The Paris Crew in action
Courtesy of New Brunswick Sports Hall of Fame

Excitement rose and fell over the surging crowd as they watched the official tug with the race umpires and the referees take up position beside the starting buoys.

Then suddenly the excitement came to a peak as the pink-shirted Saint John crew arrived on the scene. The great cheer echoed across the countryside and then died away, only to rise with a billowing sound as the crowd welcomed the English crew.

As the seconds ticked closer to 7:30 a.m. both crews began to get into their shells for the strenuous six-mile race for the four-man rowing championship of the world.

The eyes of all the spectators were on the two crews. They were well aware of the facts and figures surrounding the Paris Crew but many had to be told about the Tyne crew. They had to be told that the English boat was named *Queen Victoria*, while its crew consisted of Renforth, the captain, with his three mates, Kelly, Chambers and Percy.

The atmosphere was tense as the crowd eagerly and impatiently watched the sculls being backed up to their respective buoys. Then over the water came the voice of Hon. Thomas R. Jones, the referee: "Gentlemen, are you ready?" And then the quick reply: "We're ready!" from the captains of the two crews. "Go!" was the cry of the referee and a shout was carried through the crowd: "They're away!"

The eight oarsmen dipped their oars in the water, sending their shells shooting ahead with the terrific power of the first stroke. Fulton opened up with forty-four strokes a minute while Renforth started a steady forty-two. They carried on almost at the same clip.

Suddenly, as the boats rounded a bend in the river the spectators could see the pink shirts of the Paris Crew and the air was wild with excitement. There was only a quarter of a mile to go but the Tyne crew increased the number of strokes. Then, most dramatically in the midst of a driving surge, and, with only one hundred yards to go, the Tyne shell was seen to swerve with a mis-stroke and the crowd groaned. With a superhuman burst of energy and speed they made up the lost distance, but at that point the crowd saw the English captain, Renforth, crumpled in the stern of the boat, while the remaining three sought to fight it out.

The Paris Crew darted across the finish in the record time of 38 minutes, 50 seconds for the six-mile course, amid a wild ovation from the crowd. The large gathering turned on the Tyne Crew thinking they had

The collapse of James Renfoth into Kelly's arms
— Courtesy of New Brunswick Sports Hall of Fame

thrown the race. Cries of: "Fraud!" could be heard as they ran toward the English boat.

But the insinuations were short-lived. There was a sudden silence and an air of respect crept over the entire gathering, for James Renforth, captain of the Tyne Crew, had been stricken. He was placed in a coach and taken to the quarters of the crew nearer town. As the carriage passed through the crowds he appeared unconscious and paid no heed to the many mournful utterances of the spectators.

He was driven rapidly to his quarters at the Clairmount House. As he was being lifted from the vehicle he partially recovered consciousness and said: "Lay me down here on the grass boys, anywhere, for I feel very bad, I am sick."

They carried him into the house. A few minutes later James Renforth died in the arms of one of his crewmen.

News of Renforth's death spread widely and the Saint John victory celebration was cancelled, and the flags in the city and harbour were lowered to half-mast. And news of his death produced a great sensation in England where all were waiting for news of the race. When the body returned home the whole country mourned the passing of this great sportsman - for James Renforth was the greatest oarsman in the British Isles.

It was in honour of the English captain that the community of Renforth, New Brunswick, received its name.

For many years after that memorable race, the Renforth Regatta was an annual event to honor the Paris Crew and James Renforth - as well as an attempt to re-stimulate interest in the sport of rowing.

A Taste of Tart's

by Bill Thorpe

Many readers will remember Tart's as the hot dog stand near the Arctic Rink (burned 1939) on the site of the present Fredericton Public Library opposite the Carleton St. Armouries. I remember it well as a member of the local militia (Carleton & York Regt.) where most nights after parades in the early 1950's I would stop in for a cup of excellent coffee and a tasty hot dog or hamburg.

Tart Titus (the owner) had a sign on the building which read HYSAC COFFEE & SYMWASO HOT DOGS. He also had a reputation of being a wit and raconteur, and I often wondered what the capitalized words meant. I finally passed them off as nonsense statements. However, a more recent assessment might cause one to think otherwise. According to some sources, the sign meant: HYSAC - Here You See All Canadians and SYMWASO - Spend Your Money with Anglo-Saxons Only.

A letter has been brought to my attention sent by a V. Matthews (Scribe, York County) to George E. Davies, King Kleagle of the Invisible Empire, Knights of the Ku Klux Klan of Kanada in membership of Tart Titus, Imperial #7143, as a paid-up member of the Klan until September 30, 1930.

Such mumbo-jumbo clothed in secretiveness was a definite feature of the Klan. Quite clearly, there was more to this sign than met the eye.

Winter Horse Races at Gagetown

told by Tom Scovil

Harness racing in the winter time was a popular sport in New Brunswick in days gone by. One of the most popular racing tracks was in Gagetown where the ice would be 2 feet thick on the Saint John River by January. Saturday afternoons were a ritual for the races which were a quarter of a mile in length.

On the race day the streets of Gagetown would be a beehive of activity. Enthusiastic spectators would come from places like Fredericton, Saint John, and Moncton, as well as the locals.

In those days if there was a lot of snow down, the ice would be ploughed using heavy horses from Reid's lumber company hooked up to a grader - it was that simple.

We used to have a special name for the race horses - we called them "ice horses" because they could get over the ice quite well. It was no easy task for them. Generally the horses were matched up the best they could be with others in terms of abilities. In the early years as many as six would race at once but in the latter years most races were with only 2 horses. Of course there were a few side bets on the sly.

I reckoned it was not as dangerous on the ice as on land because if a horse took a tumble, it would just slide on the ice, no worse for wear. The horses were all sharp-shawed in any one of a number of quality blacksmith shops found here at the time. The horses also had two front and heel corks. When the horses took off it was a spectacle to behold with ice-chips spewing in all directions.

41

I remember a special two-horse race. This local horse named Jeffery, owned by Holly Bridges, was cleaning house on the other competition. Earle MacDonald, a Frederictonian, issued a challenge. He would race his horse T.J. Devlin against Jeffery with each party putting up a $200 stake with the winner taking all. Well Tom Holmes drove T.J. Devlin to the win. I know there must have been 200 people in attendance.

I remember one other time the Gagetown Driving Club brought down 5 or 6 horses from the Woodstock - Centreville area on a freight train fully equipped with a stove. They unloaded the horses at the siding and everybody came out to watch the procedure. That week, there were two afternoons of racing.

The famous Earle Avery from Knowlesville, near Woodstock, N.B., used to come here to race. He eventually became employed by the renown Woolworth brothers in the United States. He held seven world record performances. He was also inducted into the New Brunswick Sports Hall of Fame in 1976. When the Mactaquac Dam came into existence in June 1968, the races unfortunately ceased because the ice couldn't be trusted.

Memories from Frank Shute

Frank Shute, as owner operator of Shute's jewellery, was a well-known Fredericton businessman. He was also an ardent salmon fisherman as well as an outfitter of Sutter Lodge located 5 miles upriver from Doaktown on the banks of the mighty Miramichi. Here are a few more of Frank's recollections:

****

One evening we were sitting there at Big Hole Brook Camp. We heard these fellahs whoopin' and hollerin'. They were takin' fish down at Russel Rapids about a quarter mile downriver. I said as just a matter of conversation, "The guy that owned that property should do all right for catching salmon with it." Someone spoke up, "Doesn't so and so own it?" Another fellah said, "No, it belongs to some lady up in Campbellton." I said, "Oh, I see."

Well before you could say Jack I stood up and headed right down to the phone pay station in Doaktown and called a lawyer friend I knew. I said, "Do you know a Mrs. so and so?" He replied that she lived right across the street from him. I said, "Could you go across and ask her if she owned the property right across from me on the Miramichi? If she says yes, would you ask her if she'd like to put a price on it." The lawyer enquired as to the acreage involved. I told him that I understood that there was a block of ground, with a right of way to the river and the islands.

Ted Williams, Frank Shute, Vincent O'Donnell, Harry O'Donnell   ca. 1954

The next morning he called me back, named a price and said, "How does that sound to you?"

I told him to pay her and get the deed registered. That's how we did things in those days. A man's word was good as gold.

About a week later I received the title and went down to check out my new property with a friend. There was just a haze of fishing lines in the air. There were over 40 fishermen there. My friend said, "Frank, you might own the rights to this pool but you will never get to fish it."

So anyway time went on, and I went down and talked to some of the fishermen. I told them that we were going to do this the same way as they did at the Big Hole Camp. "All I ask is that the days we are here with sports, leave us alone," I said, "You know and I know the fish aren't going to wait for me." Well they were pretty good about it. The worst offenders were the people from town - Fredericton. They wanted to come over and take over the whole place. Eventually things got straightened out.

****

I remember this one older gal that came up from Atlanta, Georgia. Her husband had been a commanding officer of the Springfield arsenal. Somebody called me and said there was a lady who wanted to try her hand at salmon fishing. I thought Mr. Munn, my trusted guide at Big Hole, would be just the man to look after her. The boat he generally used was a 20 or 22 foot dug-out canoe. I reckoned she wouldn't be too comfortable in that boat, so I sent a beautiful 20 foot Chestnut Ogilvie canoe down to use. Well the bottom of that Ogilvie was as flat as the bottom of the floor. Poor Mr. Munn had an awful time getting used to it. I know the first time he took it out he fell right out of it.

He took the missus out and in a matter of no time, she missed a fish. She said, "Here you take it and try." Mr. Munn took the rod and gave it a try. It wasn't too long before he had a salmon on. He tried in vain to pass the rod to her. She would have no part of it. She asserted, "You caught it - you land it." That's the way she operated. If she didn't hook em', she didn't play them. She came back several years. I always remember her as a great old gal and a great sport.

* * * * * * *

I used to have a deal with a Mr. Hoyt that owned Big Hole Brook. In the summertime when the river warmed up the fish would pool up in the cold water pools. Big Hole was and still is a phenomenal holding pool. The principal camp for Mr. Hoyt was down in Blissfield. Up here at Big Hole there was just a little shack with a caretaker.

Dr. MacDonald from Blissfield met old Mr. Hoyt and he came back with a lot of money for those days, the early 30's. Together, they bought up properties up and down the river. I mean you have to remember that times were tough back then. It wasn't hard for Dr. MacDonald to go in to see some guy and say, "Joe, I can get you some money for that river front out there." He and Mr. Hoyt bought up properties and leases on the Miramichi, Renous, the Dungarvon, all over the place.

Eventually Mr. Hoyt built a big lodge with a sleeping camp and I was out of luck so far as Big Hole was concerned.

After Mr. Hoyt passed away the only relative interested in the properties was the daughter-in-law. She raised poodle dogs. Eventually the kennel manager and her veterinarian ended up with all the Hoyt properties. They ended up at my camp with a suitcase full of deeds and leases. They wanted to know if there was anything I'd be interested in. I did purchase the right of way over the southside parcel of land so I could ferry across in the spring. You wouldn't believe the amount of properties in that suitcase.

Golden Memories of my Canadian Literacy and Book Tour, February - October 1999

In life sometimes you have to dare to dream a dream and follow it. I did just that when I embarked on what turned out to be a 20,000 kilometer Canadian Literacy and Book Tour, from February to October of 1999. I hoped to break even in terms of cost. I received a small grant from the New Brunswick government, which included accommodation for 5 nights and a few hundred dollars for gas and posters.

Some of my friends thought I was off my rocker, while some said "Go for it - you only live once." My wife reluctantly decided to accompany me, after a little begging and pleading on my part. I approached the media in my hometown and got very little exposure. I even told some television stations that I would be featured nationally before the trip was finished. You have to be positive, and so I set out on a song and a prayer, hoping for the best.

Initially I covered New Brunswick, as many schools that would have me as well as libraries and senior-citizens homes - wherever people gathered. My first stop was on February 12 at Douglas Elementary School, the oldest continuously operating school in New Brunswick (since 1873). I travelled to such places such as Stanley, Boiestown, Moncton, Doaktown, Florenceville, Cambridge Narrows and Fredericton, regaling the audiences with stories from our province's rich heritage. Some stories involved humor, and some involved legends, but mostly they were true stories about some of our heroes, as well as some history of what it was like in days gone by.

A couple of humourous incidents come to mind. I told a junior high school class in Doaktown about a game the men played in the lumber camp called hot-ass. They thought that it was hilarious. I heard one young boy say to his friend, "that would be a neat game to play on a Friday night." One other grade 3 student at Marysville came up to me after I had told the Dungarvon Whooper story and said that when I whooped, I scared her so bad she almost had a heart attack. I told her that she was much too young for that to happen, but I thought it was pretty cute. Some schools such as the Fredericton High School English department gave me around 100 students for an hour. I was a little leery at first, but the kids really enjoyed the stories and were quite surprised and shocked to learn things that had happened essentially in their back yard - like Willie O'Ree being the first African-American to play in the National Hockey League, the world-famous Chestnut Canoe, and some of the town's legendary characters and places. I always try to bring in some humor at the start of a session to put the audience at ease. I even sang a few songs from my boyhood days at Camp Magaguadavic. I try to do some character voices from some of the stories, and have some memorized. I remember that Pat (Sharpe) Dingwall, an English teacher, laughed so hard she cried at the Quacker jokes. She also shed a few nostalgic tears as I read my memories of being a camper at Magaguadavic Lake because she, too, attended the camp as a young girl.

The principal motivation behind my writing is to keep the New Brunswick stories alive and to share them with as many people as possible. When children, adults or seniors tell me that they enjoyed the show, it is very rewarding.

With New Brunswick out of the way, plans were made for a Newfoundland and Nova Scotia trek. Of course, many phone calls had to be made for reservations and bookings. Well, my wife and I had always wanted to go to Newfoundland, and that part of the tour fit those plans to a T.

On Monday August 16, Sylvie and I set out in our Ford Windstar van for our first stop - the Canso Causeway in Nova Scotia. En route I managed to sell 32 books to the Chapters bookstore in Moncton. That was a great start, but who knew what the road ahead would bring?

Clark at North Sidney, N.S.

The next day we headed to Argentia, Newfoundland, taking the 12-hour ferry from North Sydney. I wouldn't wish that ride on anyone. The ferry was more than a little bumpy, though it's nearly as big as a Carnival cruise ship. We stayed in the day-nighter section, which was too hot and dry for my taste. People bedded down on the carpeted floor or attempted to sleep if possible in their chairs. I never slept a wink and prowled all night like a house cat.

The next morning we arrived at Argentia around 5 a.m.. Our first visual impressions of Newfoundland was that it definitely was rocky, and a person wouldn't have to be a rocket scientist to see why it has the nickname "The Rock". We proceeded through the countryside, and arrived at the Memorial University residence called Curtis House where we were to spend our 3 days. It was early in the morning, and I struck out for a little P.R.. My first stop was Tim Hortons. The first peculiarity I noticed was that all mugs of coffee came with a real spoon lying across the top. I'd never seen that before. It's no big deal, but I thought that it was different. I went to the *St. John's Telegram* newspaper, and got a nice write-up the next day. I tried C.B.C. television, but they weren't too receptive. Next I hit the Coles book stores at the Avalon and Village Malls. The next day I went to the most popular radio station, VOCM, and was granted an interview. Things were looking up.

In the afternoon we decided to play the tourist and drive the Irish-loop. Our first stop was Cape Spear, the most easterly point in North America.

We ate lunch at Witlass Bay in a little restaurant called Captain Murphy's, dining on great fish and chips. At the restaurant we noticed something strange - a blown-up brown paper bag hanging down, tied up by a string. Naturally we were quite curious as to why. The waitress told us that the bag imitates a wasp nest and house flies will not come near the place. We got chewin' the fat and the girl told us that in this little community theft and crime were very uncommon. She explained that everyone knows everyone, and house burglary is non-existent.

As we travelled along the trail we spotted a few caribou. At beautiful and picturesque Petty Harbour, two movies - "Orca" and "A Whale for The Killing" - were filmed. A bit further along I spotted some fishermen at a place called St. Vincent's. I got out and started talking to one of the locals. He told me that the body of water was called Hollywood Pond, and that it was over 100 feet deep. I spotted a sort of rock barrier on the pond beside the shore with some good-sized fish lying in it half dead.

I said, "What are they?"

He replied, "Oh, them's cod fish. Against the law to keep em', ya know." They had around three or four in the 4-6 pound class. They were catching them on spinning gear using red devils. The guy informed me, "They're goin' to be supper for someone unless the game warden comes along!" Well, I caught the drift of what was taking place. The same guy stated, "At night ya can't get near this place. I've seen eleven people comes to get their cod."

Just then a lady angler snagged into one around 6 lbs. and brought it to shore. Before I left, I got the fellah to heft up the biggest cod for a photo. As I was leaving he yelled, "Don't shows that picture to anybody cause they'd throw me in jail and takes me car!"

Well, I assured him that I wouldn't, but I added that his adventure might make it into a story published someday. The cod fishery might be shut down in Newfoundland, but they're still catchin' a few at St. Vincents - and I've got the pictures to prove it.

So far along the route, we had met no moose. But there were lots of dogs along the road which you have to pay attention to. Two quick observations to date: the gas prices are the highest in the country; the people are extremely friendly and helpful. There are breathtaking views of the ocean, with tiny villages and small dory boats nestled in coves. The accents and language are unique. It's always "yes, dear" or "yes, ma dear". And the bumps on the road are referred to as "yes mams".

That evening at Coles in Avalon Mall I sold a grand total of one book. The traffic was good, but no one knew me from Adam, and no one seemed interested in New Brunswick books. Herb Curtis, a well-known New Brunswick author, had experienced the same reaction.

The next day Sylvie and I walked downtown for a scenic tour. At 10:30 a.m. I met Mark Blackburn from C.B.C. radio, and did an interview for his Sunday - morning show.

In the afternoon I sold a few books in Coles at the Village Mall. In the evening at 7 p.m. I entertained at the Arts and Culture Centre on campus.

On Friday, August 20 we awoke bright and early and headed for Gander. Our first stop was Brigus, where I talked with a gentleman named Tom King. He informed me that he and his 17 siblings had been brought

Clark and Tom King at Brigus, NFLD

up here. Well, I couldn't imagine the hardships they must have endured as a family nor the amount of fish the family must have consumed. Today Tom works in the fish-processing plant when crab season is open. He also said that the cod fishing season was just around the corner. He said, "If I goes out and catches 11 cod and the limit is only 10 and I brings them all back and I gets caught by the warden, I'm in serious trouble. So's you got to watch yerself." In Brigus we visited the home of the famous Newfoundland sea captain Bob Bartlett, a pioneer in leading expeditions to the Arctic.

When we arrived in Gander we went to eat supper at Greco Pizza. My wife and I thought the waitress's response was kinda cute when I asked her for directions to the library. She politely informed me, "You goes down this here street - right. Then you comes to a set of lights - right. Then you turns right - right. When you comes to the fire-station you takes yer first left - right. It's down that street, not far on yer right - right. It's real easy to find - right."

I looked at my wife in bewilderment, and managed "That sounds pretty easy to find, ma dear, thanks."

That night we pitched our tent at the Country Motel and Trailer Park. The next morning I struck up a conversation with my neighbour, a Martin Elliot from St. Anthony's. He asked me if I knew where the purest water in the world could be found. I told him that I didn't have a clue. He offered my wife and me a fine sample from his cooler, and he informed us that each year he and his buddies go out and cut chunks of ice off the iceberg flows. That, he assured me, was the best water because the ice is almost free of contaminants. He also gave me detailed instructions for making the Newfoundland delicacy called "fishes and brewis" (pronounced brews).

In the afternoon I did a reading at the Gander Public Library. Afterwards a fellow named Dave told me that when Prince Charles visits Newfoundland he regularly stays at the Albatross Motel. Well, one morning at breakfast the Prince thought that he would be adventurous, and ordered the "fish and brewis". The waitress brought him a well-rounded plate which the cook had prepared especially for the Prince. Charles took one look and gasped, "I'm not a lumberjack, you know!"

August 22 and we were on the road bright and early for St. Anthony's. We crossed into Gros Morne National Park, and we were spellbound by its splendour - deep forests, majestic mountains, breath-taking fjords, and crystal blue lakes.

We stopped at a place called Daniel Harbour to get gas. The attendant was around 70 years of age. We got talking about salmon fishing in near-by rivers in days gone by. He asserted, "When I used to guide, if a sport never had a rod in his hands before, there would be no trouble to hook 20 salmon on a trip. It sure ain't like that today. I'd be lucky to get 8 in a season today."

Late that afternoon we landed at "The Triple Falls" campground. It had the cleanest washrooms you could imagine. That evening for entertainment we journeyed to a Viking dinner theatre in St. Anthony, where the only eating utensil was a spoon. The ambience, with the rough tables and garb of the actors, reflected the world of the Vikings who landed at L'Anse aux Meadows in Newfoundland 1000 years ago. Also present was a convoy of Americans from around 50 R.V.'s , who stated that Newfoundland was one of the best-kept secrets in North America. We echoed similar sentiments.

The next day we headed to the Grenfell Handicraft Store, where I sold some of my books. We also toured the historic home of Sir Wilfred Grenfell. Grenfell established a mission and schools on the Northern Peninsula and encouraged the development of a cottage-craft industry, especially rug hooking. Today the original Grenfell rugs are coveted throughout the world. A monument to his memory reads, "Real joy comes not from ease or riches or from the praise of men, but from doing something worthwhile."

We also saw our first iceberg off the coast of St. Anthony in a place called Iceberg Alley. That evening I did a reading at the St. Anthony Public Library.

The next morning we headed for L'Anse Aux Meadows on the tip of Newfoundland's Northern Peninsula, where Lief Erickson arrived around 1000 A.D.. The site now has a historical re-creation of the original settlement. Later we made our way to St. Barbe, and then took the Northern Princess ferry to Blanc-Sablon on the Labrador Coast to Labrador. We travelled around 80 kilometers up the coastline to Red Bay, the northernmost community we could access.

We dined at the Whaler's Restaurant. The fisherman's platter was unbelievable - lots of scallops, salmon and halibut. There weren't any rooms available, so we stayed in a building with a loft affording a splendid view - an orange sunset shimmered on the water overlooking the bay. After having tented for 2 days, we got a good night's sleep.

The next day we went back to the island of Newfoundland and stayed at a Bed- and-Breakfast called the J and J Hospitality Home. I sold 3 books to the owners, almost paying for the night's accommodation. We inquired about the many gardens we had passed beside roads and main highways, 15-20 miles from the nearest house. The hosts told us that local people lay claim to those areas, where they planted vegetables - mostly potatoes. Our hosts added that there's no need to protect the gardens from theft.

Moving back down the Northern Peninsula, the next day we ventured to Broom Point. We visited an old fishing home and shed that have been turned into historical sites. They had belonged to the Mudge family up to 1975. What is remarkable is that three sets of husbands, wives and children would live together in such a tiny house during the fishing season. And, mind you, it is a marvel that the families could have gotten along as one unit.

On Friday, August 27, I did an interview in Cornerbrook for the *Western Star* paper. My next stop was the Royal Bank. I arrived there a few minutes before the bank would open, so I struck up a conversation with a guy named Bill. He was dressed for work in his whites. He gave me a good quote from Joey Smallwood about Cornerbrook and its people. Joey used to say "We's the city in Newfoundland that has the cow that gives the milk." Bill also made quite a statement about the new ski resort at Marble Mountain: "It's the only place where you can ski on it Monday, skate on it Tuesday, and canoe down on Wednesday."

Our next stop was Stephenville, where I went to meet the reel doctor Larry. His business slogan reads "Don't let the big ones get away cause your gear ain't up to par!"

We then headed to the only two true French communities in Newfoundland - St. George and Grand Terre. My wife had a chance to use her French in the restaurant during dinner. That evening we stayed at a B. & B. at Port Aux Basques.

On Saturday August 28 we took the 6-hour ferry to North Sydney. We both left Newfoundland with a touch of sadness because we'd thoroughly enjoyed our stay. We vowed that we would come back sooner rather than later.

We decided to take the Cabot Trail on a whim because we had been there a few years before, and had enjoyed it. My wife did most of the driving because I am afraid of heights. She also did most of the sight-seeing from the lookouts. I did my best, and managed to really enjoy the drive. In the afternoon we arrived at Cheticamp, home of the famous Cheticamp rug hookers. One of the most famous living rug hookers is Elizabeth Lefort, whose work commands top-notch dollars.

We stayed at a campground for the night. The next day we headed to the Garden View Bed & Breakfast in Halifax. The following morning I went to ATV to do a live presentation on Breakfast Television. That afternoon I went to St. Vincent's Seniors Home for a 2 p.m. engagement. Then it was on to Chapters for the evening. The next evening an old friend, Glenn Bonnar, came to my reading at the Micmac Mall. We used to call him "Eddie Shack" when he was playing minor hockey in Fredericton.

On Thursday, September 2, my wife and I drove back to our final stop in the Maritimes - the Moncton Chapters. When that was over, we found that the tour had certainly played both of us out. However, we had a little over two weeks to recuperate before heading west.

On September 19, I felt like Julius Caesar setting out on a grand campaign, not knowing what the road ahead would bring. The first night we stayed in Granby, Quebec with Sylvie's sister, Louise, and the next day the three of us ventured into Montreal, as I had been booked at Chapters for 7 p.m.. We shopped a bit, and went to see the gigantic Eaton's store. Although it had been a central landmark, it was preparing to close its doors liquidating its stock. The three of us looked around for bargains and then I left the ladies to do their thing.

Two of my friends who lived in Brossard were also coming to meet me later on, at the reading. Wandering around on the second level of Eaton's, there completely by chance, I came across those two friends - Richard and Carol Ann Kitchen. A city with a population of over three million, and here were my old friends. It was like finding a needle in a haystack. They also came to supper with us.

That evening at Chapters we had a great audience, and I was asked to come back again.

The next morning I drove to the French newspaper of Granby, *La Voix de l'Est*, and was granted an interview. I also managed to book two sessions in an English-speaking school, Parkview Elementary. The paper came, took a photo, and did an excellent write-up. Sylvie's family were very surprised to see me in their paper.

On September 22 Sylvie and I left Granby for three morning presentations with Carol Ann Kitchen in Brossard at the Harold Napper School.

In the afternoon we motored directly to Nepean, in greater Ottawa, and the home of my sister and her husband, Pat and George Wright. Around 4 p.m. I called an old St. Thomas hockey teammate who is a bit of a character, Peter Gormley. He used to be the only guy in the AUAA to wear white skates, and he once came to a game with half his beard shaved. He told me that he was teaching in an alternative school for high school students, so I agreed to go and do a couple of sessions the next morning at the Norman Johnston Secondary School. The students were A-1 with me. Of course, they didn't have to work! In the afternoon I went to Robertson House, a seniors complex. We all had some good laughs and a lot of fun.

On the 24th I went to Briargreen Elementary in Nepean to do two morning sessions. The kids were angels and didn't want me to leave, so I stayed extra time for both classes. They were intrigued with our N.B. stories. In the afternoon I did one session with the whole school, I believe, in the gymnasium at the Leslie Public School.

During my Ottawa stay, I also visited three Chapters stores, and participated in Ottawa's "Word on the Street" - an event which was attended by thousands of people.

Then it was on to Canada's largest city, Toronto. Thank goodness Sylvie guided me to the Grange Motel - near Chinatown, in the heart of Toronto - or I would never have made it. I am not the best at finding my way around big cities. That evening I called a few friends, and Sylvie and I dined on a fine meal in Chinatown.

The next day we walked around downtown Toronto. I managed to get a few orders for books from some stores, one of which called itself "The World's Largest Bookstore".

What can you say about the streets of downtown Toronto? Well, when you are raised in a small town like Fredericton, you could sum it up as "It's a jungle out there!" In Chinatown the smells of fish and other foods could be - to put it mildly - overwhelming. On every block there are homeless men, women, boys, and girls panhandling. You see people that actually make their homes in the street. Coming face to face with these people makes you realize the seriousness and helplessness of their situation. I studied one girl in her late twenties sitting on a step, staring into space. She was definitely a lost soul. Sometimes those of us in mainstream society don't realize how good our lives are. It reminds me of the story of the person who cried because he had no shoes, until he met a man who had no legs. I don't have a remedy, but the sheer number of lost souls makes you stop and wonder.

The streets have a carnival-like atmosphere, with buskers performing for a little change. Thousands of people are milling about the sidewalks, hustling and bustling about. Tourists stand out like a sore thumb.

On Front Street, mobile concession stands sell hot dogs, hamburgs, fries, pop, and ice-cream to a fast-paced economy on the move. People with name tags, some wealthy, some not, some wannabe executives, some joggers. Each person is making his or her way in life.

The whole scene is quite overwhelming. However, I did think that the drivers in Toronto are more courteous than in those Montreal. My personal opinion - and I have been there often enough - is that many Montreal drivers think that cars have the right of way over pedestrians, and that stop signs are just yield signs. I saw a documentary on C.B.C. television that backs this up. If you don't believe it, check it out the next time you are there.

On September 29 I did a reading at the Ryerson Community Public School - just a hop, skip and jump away from the motel. It was a real eye-opener to experience so many different ethnic backgrounds in the school. I am certain that many come from low-income families. I am 100 percent certain that some had difficulty understanding English, so I spoke slower than usual and made an effort to enunciate clearly. The children were very courteous and attentive.

In the evening Sylvie and I braved a torrential downpour, and headed to the Bayview Chapters. Some of my old friends from Fredericton came, including Ted Noble - a former high school classmate, who used to play pool with me by the hour at the Cue 88, as well as Jason Perkins and Leigh White whom I coached on the rugby team at Fredericton High School, 1987 - 88.

The next day, September 30, I headed out to the parking lot with our two suitcases at 4:30 a.m.. I saw a heavy-set guy looking around the parking lot, and figured that there was going to be trouble. He approached me, and asked me if the van with the N.B. license plate was mine. I told him that it was, but he was still drawing a bead on me. I looked over my shoulder as I put the suitcases in, suspecting the worst. He passed me by as I jumped into the van, and drove around front to pick up my wife. I told the desk attendant about the incident. He told me that the person I encountered was security. How would you ever know seeing he was in civies?

After Toronto, our next stop was Sault Ste. Marie, which seemed an unusually long drive. An old friend of mine whom I chummed around with in Fredericton in 1978 lived there. He had once been a first-rounder in the N.H.L., and a great person. I had always wondered what he was up to. I called his mother. To my shock and dismay, she told me that he had committed suicide. So often in life we fail to keep in contact with our old friends and live to regret it.

The next morning we were on the road again — destination Thunder Bay. We spent a couple of days there and I did another reading at Chapters.

We went from the woods to the prairies and after several long hours on the road, arrived at Winnipeg. On the 5th of October I went to the Lincoln Middle School. The first two classes I talked to enjoyed the session so much that their teachers wanted me to stay for an extended session with another group. I thought that was a great compliment, and told them 'no problem'. I think there were 125 students in total in the second group.

The next day I went to the Ness Junior High School. I also was booked into Chapters for two evenings.

On October 7 I approached *The Leader Post* in Regina for a write-up. They were great, and the next day I got some press. That evening we found ourselves back in Chapters, where I was given a message to call the Montreal-based C.B.C. television program *Culture Shock*. One of their reporters, Patrice Fombelle, wanted to do a feature on me. He'd apparently read about me in *La Voix de l'Est*, and wanted to come to Calgary. Needless to say, I was elated. Good things were going to happen!

On October 9 the van was speeding towards Edmonton. My sister Shirley and her husband, John Duncan, were to be our hosts for around a week in St. Albert, 15 minutes from Edmonton. On October 11 John took us on an excursion to Jasper in the Rocky Mountains and in particular, to a little place called the Miette Springs. We went for a stroll in the mountains. The air was cool and crisp with a great forest scent. When we got back from our hike, we went to the hot-springs pool. The water was unbelievably warm, and a sign warned bathers not to stay in more than 20 minutes. That was time well spent and I highly recommend it. When you come out of the pool, you feel like a million bucks.

Afterwards we went for a bite to eat. I got talking to the waitress and enquired, "Any grizzly bears around here?" She replied, "No. Not around here. There might be some around 30 miles down the road." I jokingly remarked, "We probably have more grizzly bears back home in New Brunswick than you do around here." "Probably," she said. Imagine!

On October 12 I visited the Chateau Mission, a seniors' residence in St. Albert. I got a photo and a nice write-up in the *St. City News*.

The next morning I visited Glendale Elementary School, and in the evening it was back to Chapters at the West Edmonton Mall. For anyone who has never seen the mall, it is humongous! It even has a skating rink, which I tried twice. Stewart MacDougal, a former Frederictonian, showed up at the reading. He makes his living as a singer-songwriter, and has recently released an excellent CD called *"Gathering Time"*.

On October 14 it was over to Keenoo Shayo Elementary School. In the evening, it was another Chapters book-signing. Sales were encouraging.

After bidding adieu to our hosts, we made a beeline straight to Calgary. Along the highway the Rocky Mountains stand tall to the right, a foreboding presence. You can see them from 60 miles away. We settled in with one of my closest friends, Larry Goodine, together with his wife, Connie and their children. That evening at Chapters was like old-home week, full of old friends from down east. Even my long lost blood-brother, Blane Little, showed up.

The next morning around 11 a.m. Patrice Fombelle arrived from Montreal to shoot a documentary for the C.B.C. television program *Culture Shock*. After three days of filming, he eventually called the piece "The New Brunswick Apostle".

The first day he shot rolls of film at locations around Calgary. In the afternoon we arrived at the West Hills Branch of Chapters. This was the largest turnout to date. Patrice filmed everything. That evening a group of us went to Stromboli's for Italian food. Patrice told us that he had been leery of Calgarians, and expected some red-neck treatment because of his French background. Instead, he said the people had been very friendly and courteous. That evening of the 6 of us, 4 spoke French, so he felt right at home.

On Sunday at 2 p.m. I had my last reading at a Calgary Chapters on the McLeod Trail. Word must have spread because there was a fantastic, enthusiastic crowd. I sold 32 books at the reading, so I was more than pleased. Patrice, once again, filmed every minute detail. That evening I got to see a Calgary Hitman major junior hockey game at the Saddledome. We had great seats after shelling out 15 bucks each. Calgary defeated Kamloops, 6-3.

McLeod Trail Chapters in Calgary, Alberta

On October 18 Patrice, Sylvie and I visited the Monsignor Doyle Elementary School - grades 3 and 5. The first question Patrice asked the children before I entered the room was, "What do you know about New Brunswick?" And of course one cute little red-haired girl, looking perplexed, announced "Nothing!" After I left he interviewed some of the children again, and got some positive responses. Patrice was a super guy, a gentleman and a great guy to work with. His 5 ½ minute documentary showed across Canada in bilingual form approximately every 10 weeks during the year 2000.

After the filming was complete, we bid Patrice farewell and headed for British Columbia. To say that driving into the Rockies is spectacular is an understatement. It is like entering another planet, foreboding and truly awesome. I should mention that I have a fear of heights, so you know who did most of the driving. We took the Trans-Canada, the scenic route. When we got to Fraser Canyon, there was a sign saying "This awesome gorge has always been an obstacle to transportation. Indians used ladders, and road builders hung "shelves" to skirt its cliffs. Canoes rarely dared its whirlpools; only one stern wheeler fought it successfully. Railyards and highways challenged it with tunnels and bridges, but today man and nature still battle for supremacy." (Province of British Columbia 1966). By the time we got to Hell's Gates, I could barely get out of the car. I sure couldn't look down.

The Rockies

On the second day we came down into the Okanogan Valley, and it too was like visiting another country. There were still fruit on the apple trees, and the temperature was around 20° C. Eventually we ended up in Delta, at the residence of my uncle, Gerald Peabody and his wife Anne.

On October 20 we crossed the Twassen Ferry to Victoria. We couldn't believe the temperature there. It was around 25. We found a great Chinese restaurant for lunch, and stayed downtown at the Strathcona Hotel. The rates were very reasonable. We enjoyed strolling around downtown Victoria. That evening was to be my last Chapters stop.

The next morning we got the Royal Tour of Victoria, and a free breakfast, courtesy of my sister's friend Andy Anderson. I could easily understand why a person would want to live there.

From October 21 - 27 we stayed in Delta again with my uncle. We did a lot of sight-seeing and touring. On the 22nd we went to Vancouver to visit my brother Jim. We did a walking tour, which included the legendary

Gastown. We walked downtown to the Chinese section. My brother, a Vancouver resident of 20 years, pointed out a few areas that are unsafe because of their many drug addicts. We also had a chance to visit Stanley Park, as well as the Granville Market.

At Stanley Park there are a number of Indian totem poles. One sign explains the significance:

Indian Totem Poles

The totem was the British Columbia Indians "coat of arms". Totem poles are unique to the coast of B.C. and lower Alaska. They were carved from western red cedar, and [the] carving tells a real or mythical event. They were not idols, nor were they worshipped. Each carving on each pole has a meaning. The eagle represents the kingdom of the air, the whale, the lordship of the sea, the wolf, the genius of the land, and the frog, the transitional line between land and sea.

On Saturday, October 23 at 2 p.m. my final stop was the Vancouver Public Library. The building resembles a Roman Amphitheatre. You could get lost in it really easily. I was very pleased with the nice turnout.

The next morning we were on the road back home. Feeling brave, I took over the wheel near Rodgers Pass, which is some 14,000 feet high. I thought the worst was over. What a mistake! I took a panic attack, and had to cover my right eye so I couldn't look down driving at about 60 kilometers an hour. I would never want to experience a snowstorm in places that are marked "Danger of an Avalanche". Many lives seem to have been lost in avalanches and traffic accidents, judging by a number of white crosses we saw beside the road. Well, it makes you wonder if you are ever going to make it through alive!

Upon arriving home it took a couple of days to sink in that the ordeal was completed. I had journeyed 20,000 kilometers from one end of the country to the other, promoting literacy and sharing New Brunswick stories with many Canadians.

"If you dream it, you can do it."
- Walt Disney

his first canvas covered canoe, a Chestnut, which was to arrive by the time he would meet his first hunter. When we finished work on the McQuade camp, and the time had come when father was to go to the Forks to meet the first hunter of the season, Dr. Weller, I took him in the old canoe to Red Bank, a distance of about twelve miles. From there he walked, and I poled back to get a little more practice in canoeing. I saw my first moose that day, a bull with large antlers and also a cow. I was to wait at the McQuade camp for father and his hunter, who arrived about dark the following night, and go with them to Upsalquitch lake, the extreme farther end of their hunting territory. The next day we reached Nictau Lake, and later went over the divide to Nepisiguit Lakes, coasted down the swift Nepisiguit River to Portage Brook, and over a six mile portage to a little camp to the lake shore. We reached our destination about noon on the last day of August, made camp with as little noise as possible, and shortly before dark moose began to come into the lake to feed on water plants. At one time we could see eight moose, two of which had good antlers, but no attempt was made to shoot one of them, as the season would not be open until the following morning. There was an old canoe there which we used on the lake, and the canoes we came down in were left on the bank of the Nepisiguit River. I made several trips over the six mile portage to pack in supplies.

Upsalquitch Lake was about as far from civilization as one could be in New Brunswick. At that time it was necessary to go a long way in to get the best moose hunting, as the Tobique and Nepisiguit Lake regions had been raided by Indians some time in the 1880's and practically stripped of moose when their hides were in demand for making the white buckskin belts worn over the dark grey topcoats of the Canadian soldiers. In 1900, they had not fully recovered from this slaughter, and did not reach their highest numbers until about 1910.

In 1900 there were very few deer in the Tobique-Nepisiguit country, but caribou were there in great numbers. Deer increased so rapidly that by 1910 they were evidently depleting some of the food necessary to the diet of the caribou, and disease was taking such a toll of caribou that after the hunting season of 1915 a closed season was declared on them, which was never to open again. Several caribou were found dead in the woods, and I saw the last one north of Nictau Lake in November 1928. It was in the last stages of tuberculosis and walking in circles. I caught and examined it without difficulty, and the next morning it was lying dead almost in the camp yard. One buck deer and two small bull moose were found in the

Nictau Lake region about that time in a similar condition, and all were found dead later.

Caribou are the most delicate of the deer family, and therefore were the first to weaken and contract disease when the number of animals reached a point in excess of the food supply. There are now no caribou left in New Brunswick, and with their passing went also much of the disease they carried, and which both deer and moose contracted to a small extent while there were caribou to carry it.

Deer continued to increase. Unfortunately for the lordly moose there was a shortage of certain water plants necessary in the moose diet, and the king of the deer family dwindled. The hard winter of 1934 reduced the deer about fifty percent. Eventually the moose in the north regained their numbers. Each year several beautiful calves are seen, but seldom a yearling. Bears have increased, since there has been a very limited market for their pelts, and many of them have graduated from scavengers to killers, and are preying on young moose. I mention these things as my observance of them has made my Tobique experiences extremely interesting.

The Danny Grant Story

The only Maritimer to win the Calder Trophy Rookie of the year (1968-69), an Ironman, playing 566 consecutive games in the NHL, a 50-goal scorer in the NHL (1974-75), and a two-time winner of the NHL showdown Daniel Frederick Grant is truly a great Maritime hero. Born February 21, 1946, he grew up near Fredericton in the small community of Barkers Point.

The son of Jean and Fred Grant, Danny's siblings were John, Paul, Gerry, Tony, Barb and Patsy who died at an early age. Jean stayed at home to look after her family, instilling in her children the important values of caring and sharing. Fred worked at Ashley Colter Ltd. with Diamond Construction for 30 years, first as a truck driver and later in the planing mill. Then he moved to Natural Resources where he worked for 20 years. While Danny was growing up, Fred saw in his son the potential of a exceptional hockey player, although as a busy man he didn't have much time to observe his son at play.

Fred observes, "One thing I think that helped Danny was the fact that when the boys played on the outdoor rinks, they played all day, with lots of ice time. On the ponds, everybody had a chance, no matter how good they were. And on Saturday night all the kids got together to watch their heroes on Hockey Night in Canada. All the kids in the neighborhood were good kids. There was no trouble to get into. There were no drugs, hardly anyone smoked, they couldn't afford the tobacco, they all played sports. It was a different world."

Danny started playing hockey at the age of five, using his mother's skates on a little flooded pond in the back yard. He loved the game from the very beginning. He and the other kids in Barkers Point loved playing on Bird's Pond where they could skate for miles. Besides playing shinny hockey, they even played cowboys and Indians on skates with whatever equipment they could scrounge up, mostly hand-me-downs. At Christmas time, every boy hoped to get something relating to hockey. The big thing back then was to maintain a hockey stick.

Danny's brothers John and Paul, his cousins Wayne and Carl Grant, Ron Goodine, Bucky Murray, George Miles, brothers Gary and Frank, Larry Banks, Dave Jewett, Fred Holland, George McMinniman, Bob Hoyt, all were part of the Barker's Point Gang. Wayne Grant was a member of the Fredericton City Police Force until 1995 when he died of cancer. Danny observes that Bob Hoyt's sister Betty was one of the greatest natural athletes he has ever seen. The Dunphy brothers' uncle Bob was a great positive influence on many of the boys from the Point.

From grade one to grade eight, Danny attended Barkers Point School where the principal Glen Melvin started a very active hockey program. The team played exhibition games and went two years without a loss while Danny was a player. In spite of Mrs. Moore being a disciplinarian and no stranger to the use of the strap, many of the boys, including Danny, repeated grade eight so they could stay on at the school and play hockey.

From Barkers Point School, Danny went on to Devon Junior High where Glen Sandwith and Les Hull strongly supported the sports program. There was baseball, track and field in the spring and summer, a little rugby in the fall and, of course, hockey in the winter.

Outside school, Danny played minor hockey for a team called Barkers Point Bantams sponsored by Burton Colter with Charlie West as coach. Charlie says of Danny, "He didn't need a coach. I just had to open the door. He could score goals and played left wing. If I needed a goal, I could double shift Danny and put him on defence. He loved to play. Colby Fraser and Danny would stand up on the bench, they were so eager to play."

Danny's younger brother Tony was only 6 or 7 but he remembers Danny practising all the time. "Danny would set a tire up and would continually shoot pucks through it by the hour and I think his practising paid off and helped him become a goal scorer. He also worked at Bob Dunphy's lugging concrete one summer and that kept him in shape."

In those days, Danny was playing over a hundred games a season.

"When I was 14 or 15 I probably played for 7 or 8 teams," Danny recalls. "I played school boy hockey, a church league, played with Barkers Point Aces in the commercial league. I played on the Midget team, the Junior team until Christmas and the senior team as well. You always took your gear to the rink. There were always guys that didn't show up for certain teams. I remember Arnold Cream had the junior team and myself, Georgie Miles and Paul Rickard and some other guys would stand outside the rink. If they didn't have enough players to go on the road, Arnold would say, 'Get on the bus.' The cut-off signing was around January 10 to be on a team."

In Danny's first year of Midget he played for the Fredericton Hawks. Danny's father Fred remembers a playoff game against the Miramichi where Danny scored 8 goals.

Danny also played for the Fredericton Midget Bears. Laurie Menzies was the Coach and Ab MacDonald was the assistant and manager of the team.

Danny was also a rink-rat at the York Arena under Bob VanHorne. The boys used to clean the ice during the junior and senior games as well as the stands when the games were finished. Bob used to call the boys in to help out and maybe on a Sunday morning the rewards would be a couple of hours of ice- time. Danny remembers his rink-rat days as being a lot of fun.

He also remembers his first pair of quality skates: "Hardly anybody had good equipment, it was just a sign of the times. I got my first pair of CCM tacks from Junior Doherty second hand for 10 bucks. They were a size and a half too big so I just used an extra pair of socks. I wore them until I went to Peterborough where I got fitted for proper skates and they kinda chuckled over the fact that I had been playing with skates a couple of sizes too big."

Some of the older guys around town had an influence on Danny, guys like Dag Seymour, Reg Wheaton, Doc Feeney, Bev Bawn, Bob Mabie, Dick Yeomans, Neil and Doug Sewell, Richard Clark, Willie O'Ree and Knucker Irvine. Robert Grant always gave Danny a stick when he was playing Junior. These were some of the guys he looked up to.

Danny mentions playing senior hockey at age 15 and getting in a rare fisticuffs, "I got in a fight with Bill Donovan from Saint John and he pretty near killed me at the York Arena."

The Grant brothers: John, Gerry, Paul, Tony, Danny

When Danny was in grade 9 both the Montreal Canadiens and Boston Bruins contacted him saying that they wanted him to play Junior hockey. At the time Danny didn't even know what Major Junior hockey was. The only thing that Danny knew was that a team out of Moncton with Oscar Gaudet on it went to the Memorial Cup in Ottawa and got their butts kicked. Gerald Regan, a scout from Boston, and Roly McLenahan who had just retired from professional hockey and came back home from Montreal contacted Danny about playing Junior hockey.

Danny was set to go to Niagara Falls with Boston but his Dad knew Roly as they had grown up together. Roly set up a meeting in Marysville with Phil Goyette and Dickie Moore at a hockey banquet. Danny was pretty impressed so he decided to go with Montreal. Roly maintained contact with Danny throughout his career. Roly was also a tremendous athlete in his own right playing in the American Hockey League for many years and a few games in the NHL when there were only 6 teams.

Danny notes that if he had gone with the Boston Bruins that he might have ended up in the NHL 2 years earlier. Danny went with the number one team in the world at that time loaded with veteran players. He learned many a valuable lesson in life with the organization. In the long run it was the best thing that ever happened to him.

Danny talks about playing hockey in the NHL:

"Hockey is a game of skill but there are many other intangible elements that go along with it such as commitment, work and anticipation. I think that a lot of it comes from knowing and understanding the game. What separates good players is not whether they are big or strong, or they can skate, or shoot the puck but understanding the game. If you look at some great players, the guys who know how to play the game, the puck follows them around the ice. Another guy can skate a hundred miles an hour and lose 10 pounds in a game and not accomplish much. Understanding and being a student of the game are key ingredients to success."

Danny's favourite team growing up was the Montreal Canadiens. Jean Beliveau was his favourite all-time player for his contributions to hockey on and off the ice. Another favourite was Stan Mikita, strictly from his skills at playing the game. He was such a smart and intelligent player. He was just a small guy and won scoring championships. He wore #21 and

Danny followed suit throughout much of his career. But overall no one would ever come close to Jean Beliveau.

Danny says Bobby Orr was the best there ever was and there was no one who could hold a candle to him. Danny played against him all through Junior and all though the NHL. It is hard to imagine even in comparing him to Wayne Gretzky and his stats. No player ever controlled the game like Bobby Orr. Danny says that Bobby Orr could have the same success playing on a terrible team as he would on a Stanley Cup team. He could take guys on a team to another level, guys like Phil Esposito and Johnny Bucyk and Wayne Cashman. When Orr showed up in Boston as an 18-year-old kid, the play of the team just sky-rocketed. Bobby Orr could do it all. He could skate, he had a change of gears with about 4 or 5 different speeds, saw the ice like Gretzky. It was just unfortunate in those days, caution wasn't a big part of the game in protecting players. The Boston Bruins just destroyed a tremendous talent. That happened to a lot of players then. Bobby Orr won 2 scoring championships as a defenceman but he was only healthy for 7 or 8 years.

Danny left home for Peterborough at age 16, it was 1,200 miles from home. At the time four New Brunswickers were invited to training camp. Ricky Cochrane, Ronnie Vermett, George Berube and Danny. Danny was the only one to make the grade. The Peterborough Petes were the Junior team of the Montreal Canadiens. Danny remembers his first training camp,

"It was really funny when I left home for Peterborough training camp. There was nothing about calling you in to say you made the team. You just reported every day. If your name was on the door not crossed off, that meant you got the gear. There were a hundred kids in the rookie camp and a hundred at the main camp. I remember there would be like 6 teams and you would play games. Every day there would be lists on the door with names crossed off. The trainer would be there handing them the train ticket and say, 'See you later.'

One day after practice it looked like every name was crossed off. I said, 'Oh geez, I'll get back home.' I looked again and there was only one name, mine, not crossed off. Just then the trainer walked in and he said, 'You are going to the big room, you made the team, pick out what number you want and Mr. Bowman wants to see you after.' Scotty was the head scout with the Montreal Canadiens.

When I went to see him, he said, 'Have you got a suit?' I said, 'No.' He said, 'You finish up here and you and I will take a little trip.' The first place he took me was for a haircut, a brush-cut and the second place was for a new suit."

Danny started out as a 4th liner in his first year and scored 12 goals and 12 assists. Richard Scammell from Fredericton, joined the team in Danny's second year and was his roommate for 3 years. After Junior hockey Richard earned a hockey scholarship to RPI at Troy, New York.

In his second year at Christmas he had 18 goals until he had his jaw broken in two places at Christmas. Someone ran him from behind after the whistle. Danny's plans had been to meet a Marysville boy, Oscar 'Beno' Allen who was playing for Guelph Biltmores and come home together. He and Danny had been working together at the Devon Lumber Company in the previous summer. He never went home, he ended up in the hospital. Bino was killed in a car accident that same summer.

Danny came back a little bit in the playoffs wearing a special helmet that J.C. Tremblay had used in the Stanley Cup Playoffs with the Canadiens. In Danny's third year he had 48 goals and the following year 44 but he also missed games as he was called up with the pro teams in Quebec and Hull. During his last two years he was a first liner and was captain of the team in his last year.

During Danny's third year Andre Lacroix was his centre and Leo Thiffault was his right winger. Andre went on to play with Philadelphia. The trio formed the number one line in the OHL at that time. Danny played 56 games amassing 47 goals and 59 assists for 106 points. He was selected second team all-star.

In the fourth year Leo graduated and Mickey Redmond took his place. The last year the coach was Roger Bedard from outside Montreal, while Frank Mario from Cornwall coached the first 3 years Danny was there.

Danny tells what it was like playing, "In my Junior days there was a lot of fighting, it was rough but a different type of roughness than today. You didn't have the guys running you like you do today. There wasn't a lot of running from behind. When I played you didn't have face masks, mouthguards and the equipment they have today. When I played you had the best players from the Maritimes, Quebec and Ontario playing in the OHL. There were only 6 teams. Most guys on the teams could play. The Junior Canadiens had all the best players in Quebec to pick from. Today there are

16 teams in the QMJHL. Today a lot of Junior teams might not have one player go on to play in the NHL."

For Danny his Junior days were four of the most important years of his life. He was doing something that he loved, making great friends and felt connected to the community. He laughs that he had more money than he has now. He was making $30 a week. Danny said that he always managed to make a little on the side. He worked with Coca-Cola in the summer time for three summers.

Danny talks a little bit about his first year away.

"It was just something awful the first few months. You are homesick and every other day you are going to quit and go home. Then you just tough it out. At Christmas time I think we had 10 days off. After the thrill of seeing everyone and family I went back after only 8 days. I missed Peterborough so bad. I knew then that I would never be homesick again. That was what I wanted to do and this was my new family. We were all hockey players and we travelled all over Ontario and Quebec. When we went to Toronto to play we had 13-14,000 people and the same in the Forum in Montreal.

I remember when I signed my first pro contract in 1966. I was called up and Sam Pollock was sitting behind the desk with Toe Blake over in the corner. Sam was saying how pleased they were with me and he wanted to sign me to a 2-year contract. He slid me over a contract for $10,000, the same as they did for everyone else. The funny thing about it was the night before Mickey Redmond and I had rehearsed our refusal to take not a cent less than a certain amount and we were as brave as could be.

I told Sam, 'No, I am not happy with that.'

Sam said, 'What do you think you are worth?'

I said, 'I think I should be making around $25,000 a year.'

I didn't say anything for a minute and then he speaks out, 'You think you are as good as Rocket Richard?'

I said, 'No, I wouldn't even suggest that. That's the furthest thing from my mind, it's ridiculous.'

He reached into the drawer and pulled out the contract of Rocket Richard's, the last year he played, his salary was $25,000.

I said, 'Where's the contract?' and of course I signed.

When I stood up to leave Toe Blake stood up in the corner. He said, 'Remember you are playing for the Montreal Canadiens. You get $15,000 for winning the Stanley Cup. You will make your $25,000.'

He was right. We did win the cup.

The only time that I was ever nervous was my first game in the NHL in 1966. It was televised down here in New Brunswick. I was so nervous my feet felt like lead. I received a telegram with over 400 signatures on it from fellow New Brunswickers wishing me well. I was on the number one line with Jean Beliveau and Bobby Rousseau. I only got a couple of shifts."

Later that night Danny felt pretty down about the way he played. Toe Blake recognized something was not right when Danny told him how he felt. The famous Coach and former NHL All Star said, "Don't feel bad, in my first game I was so nervous I couldn't even skate."

Danny played with Houston in 1966-67 with the Central League where he had over 20 goals up until Christmas. There were many players in the league who went on to the NHL. The team was playing in St. Louis, a farm team of Chicago with guys like Dennis Hull and Phil Esposito playing for the St. Louis team. Sam Pollock, Claude Ruel and Scotty Bowman came down to watch the game. Danny scored a hat trick but he wrapped his leg around the goal post and tore his knee. In those days the goal posts didn't move. He was supposed to go with the big club the following day. Instead he ended up in Houston in a hospital with his leg in traction. He didn't play the rest of the year.

In the next year at training camp Danny led the Montreal Canadiens with 12 goals in exhibition games and figured he made it. The brass called him in and told him that he was a big part of the future but right now you are going to Houston. Danny was disappointed at first but reported to Houston and started playing the way he could.

Finally on December 3, in 1967 he joined the Canadiens at Boston playing with Mickey Redmond and Jacques Lemaire and got 3 assists. At the time the Canadiens were really struggling, 10 points out at first. The "Kid Line" produced really well but it wasn't long before the 3 of them were in the stands. Why the younger players were brought up primarily was to send a message to the older players. At the time guys like Dickie Duff and Gilles Tremblay weren't doing the job but that soon changed.

Stanley Cup and Prince of Wales Trophy winners

ley et du trophée Prince de Galles

The team went on to win the League championship and the Stanley Cup. At the time of the playoffs Danny played primarily on checking assignments on the fourth line. He was 22 when he was on the Stanley Cup team.

"There was champagne, parades, a lot of publicity but at the time as a 22 year old it didn't seem that big of a deal. You have to remember that this was the Montreal Canadiens and you were expected to win."

On June 29, 1968 Danny married Linda Ann Simpson, eldest of 4 daughters of Bob and Olive Simpson. She remembers meeting Danny for the first time and what life was like to be married to a professional hockey player.

"I met him in the summer of 1965 in front of my father's grocery store. He was working for Bob Dunphy and was on his lunch break. I was not a hockey fan and did not know who he was. Once we started dating, hockey became a big part of my life.

Two weeks before we were married, Dan was traded to Minnesota. Life would never be the same. I was so nervous leaving home for the first time and not knowing anyone but the other hockey wives made me feel welcome. In those days wives did not travel to any away games and so we got together to keep each other company.

Over the years I took 3 wives to the hospital to have their babies because their husbands were on the road playing hockey."

Danny and Linda had 2 children, Kelly Lynn born in 1970 at Fredericton and Jeffrey Daniel was born in 1972 in Minnesota on the night of a home game. Linda remembers one of her girlfriends took her to the hospital because Dan had to go to the rink to play. In those days the guys did not get the night off even if their wife was having a baby.

Danny talks a bit about the game and being lucky:

"If things are going well in hockey you don't change a thing. Hockey players seem to have their own rituals. If I eat spaghetti at 2 o'clock and I score 2 goals then you know the next game I'll do the same thing. Some guys like to be the first on the ice or the last off. Some guys will circle the net. You have your good and bad days on the ice. The only thing about my job is that you are in front of 16,000 to 18,000 people and when you have a bad day, everyone notices it.

Linda, Jeffrey, Kelly, Danny

When I first got in the NHL we travelled by train to Detroit, Boston, Chicago, New York and Toronto. With 6 teams and a 72 game schedule there was more team camaraderie than today. Back then guys stayed on teams for years. You see what is going on today. There is no loyalty on the owner's or player's part. The train was something where you could get up and move around and socialize. I thought it was great. Gump Worsley loved the trains especially because he had a dreaded fear of flying.

Every team had their share of pranksters. For the Montreal Canadiens it was Ralph Backstrom and John Ferguson. It was hard to believe that Ferguson, who was known as one of the toughest fighters at the time in the NHL was one of the biggest pranksters you could imagine.

I remember one night as a rookie on the train, we rookies had to go get sandwiches for everybody and run back just as the train was pulling out of the station. We would throw the sandwiches through the windows and jump on the moving train. Back then the rookies couldn't associate with the veterans until they were initiated. The veterans had their room where they might have a few pops and a card game. I asked Ralph Backstrom which bunk I should take. He said, 'Take lower four.' I took the bunk and about 1 or 2 in the morning there was a tap on my shoulder. It was Big Jean Beliveau's bunk. He looked real serious and said, 'I think you're in the wrong bunk.' I didn't take long to get out of that bunk. I looked for an empty bed half the night."

The next year, 1968-69, Danny Grant and Claude Larose were loaned to Minnesota North Starts, an expansion team. Montreal had just won 4 Stanley Cups in 5 years. He was brought into the office before Toe Blake and Sam Pollock. They told him that they couldn't keep all their players.

Danny went to Minnesota the second year of expansion, 1968-69. In one way he was looking forward to going to Minnesota but his heart was still in Montreal. It turned out to be one of the best things to ever happen to him. Danny played 6 years in Minnesota, where he won the Rookie of The Year, played on 3 all-star teams and established himself as a bonafide NHLer.

When Danny won the Calder Rookie of the Year he became the highest scoring rookie in league history up until that time. He surpassed Bernie (Boom Boom) Geoffrion's record of 30 goals and Gus Bodnar's total points by scoring 34 goals and 31 assists for an astounding total of 65 points. At the awards banquet that season he was joined by some high pro-file players for the NHL Individual Trophy Awards. Alex Delvecchio won the Lady Byng Memorial, Bobby Orr, the James Norris trophy and Phil Esposito, the Art Ross and Hart trophies. Danny played on a line with Danny O'Shea and Claude Larose and formed one of the best lines in the NHL. The second year Larose went back to Montreal and Buster Harvey, from Fredericton, was drafted by the North Stars. Buster was immediate-ly put on the right side with Danny. Jude Drouin was at centre. Buster scored 22 goals and was a big reason the line was the best on the team. Bill Goldsworthy and Danny each won the team scoring title 3 times in the 6 years they played together.

Danny was honoured in Fredericton for winning the Calder Cup Rookie of the Year with a special Danny Grant Day. There was a parade through the streets of Fredericton where he signed hundreds of autographs. There was an open barbeque in Barkers Point. There was also a sign at the beginning of Greenwood Drive that read, 'Barkers Point, Hometown of Danny Grant.' Later that evening there was a reception at the Beaverbrook Rink where Linda and Danny were presented with a 14 foot fibreglass boat called Miss North Star with a 40 horse-power engine. Later on there was a dance with all the proceeds to minor hockey.

Danny talks about his career:

"I had played in Minnesota for 6 years and I thought that I would end my career there. I loved it in Minnesota but there was turmoil at the management level and it worked its way into the dressing room. I approached Wren Blair (GM) at the end of the season and asked if he would trade me. He looked at me and said, "You will never be traded as long as I am the GM of this team. I got a call from Wren in June and he said; 'Guess what! I've been fired and you have been traded to Detroit.' I said, 'I know I heard it on the radio.' Wren ended the conversation by saying that he never broke his word to me, he was fired before I was traded.

I was really excited about going to Detroit and even though they did not have a contending team, I was looking forward to playing in my favorite rink (Olympia) and reuniting with my old buddy from Peterborough, Mickey Redmond.

I started the season, 1974-75, playing with Mickey and Bill Hogaboam. Things were going well and I was on my way to a 30-

Danny and Miss North Star; 1969

35 goal year when Hogie broke his ankle and Mickey suffered a career-ending back injury. There I was with no centre or right wing. Nick Libett, who was playing on a line with Marcel, got hurt and I was inserted into his spot. It was as though we were made for each other and had been playing together all our lives. I ended up the season with 50 goals in 78 games, the 12th player in history to score 50 goals. I played with a lot of good players but I never played with anyone like Marcel Dionne who went on to score over 1,600 points in a 16-year career.

About three-quarters of the way into the season I had one of the biggest decisions of my hockey career to make. Do I go for the 50 or settle for whatever I end up with? I was 29 years old and felt that I could play for another 5-6 years if I stayed healthy and by scoring 50 goals would I be able to reach that level again or even come close to it.

I went over to Mickey's house and we talked. His advice was to go for it because you never know what's waiting for you down the road. He was right, the next year 9 games into the season my career was over. The injury was called anterior thigh rupture. I tried hockey in 1978-79 with L.A. Kings but it was in vain, I wasn't myself because of my injury. The other reason I went for it was the 'fans'. They stuck with us all year and did not have a whole lot to cheer about and I thought this would be a great way to thank them. I told Marcel the next morning that I was going for the 50 and he said 'So am I'. He ended up with 47.

On the 50th goal Marcel dumped the puck into Phil Roberto's corner. Phil went in behind the net and rubbed the guy out. I picked up the loose puck, stepped out in front of the net and shot a backhander in.

When I played hockey it was a different era and a different time. We didn't do a lot of hobnobbing with movie stars or golf legends. We chummed around with our teammates from the NHL. It would be no different from the local senior guys hanging around and enjoying each other's company. Most of the guys came from small towns. Most had to work their tails off to get where they were. Most of them played for practically nothing for years. They played under the worst circumstances you could imagine, the Eddie Shores of the world. Nobody had any great amount of money. You went out after the game and there wasn't one guy who said I'll buy the round, everybody took their turn. There was no big salary gap. We lived in apartments. There were no million dollar homes. When we got together the whole team would get together as well as the wives. We were very close-knit."

Danny Grant had his own set of rules on how he wanted to play hockey. He always wanted to do well. He always promised himself that whatever success he had at the game he would do it without trying to hurt anybody. Back then everyone was stereotyped. The coaches and management always tried to make you something you weren't. Danny's bread and butter was going to the net, taking his whacks and trying to get his stick on the puck. Today they are begging guys to go for the net. Everyone wants to go for the corners. In his day if you didn't go to the corner you were a chicken. He liked to get the puck coming out of his end. He either got the puck out quickly or found his center. He liked to come late and find the hole so he could get the puck back. His greatest strength was that he had a very accurate shot. Danny says that as a hockey player he prided himself on being able to shoot the puck and score goals. He believes for a player to make the grade at the NHL level you have to learn to do one thing really well.

"Everyone always thought that the Montreal Canadiens were the fastest skating team in the NHL. They weren't. They were the fastest puck movers. J.C. Tremblay and Jacques Laperrière, and all these guys looked like they were so fast because their puck was always in motion. The Canadiens were synonymous with speed and the speed came with transition. It is the same today with Detroit Red Wings and the Colorado Avalanche. When I played in the Original Six each team had their own system. Today the teams basically all play the same style. When I played Junior we learned the Montreal Canadiens system. When I joined the Canadiens there was no teaching systems. You had to know the system when you got there. Today in the NHL there are as many as 7 coaches with the teams who have to teach the players their system."

Danny has his own philosophy about year round hockey for youngsters:

"I think that hockey for kids year round is utterly ridiculous. People are under the impression that more is better. Most guys that ever played the game will tell you that. The kids should be allowed to play all sports, soccer, golf, baseball, whatever. Hockey is a winter sport. When I played hockey as a kid, I also played rugby, lacrosse and baseball. If someone told me that I couldn't play another sport while I was playing hockey I would have said, excuse me, because I love all sports. When I became a professional and I signed with the Montreal Canadiens and they said you are not playing lacrosse any more, then I didn't because now I was working for them and respected their wishes.

Parents have a role to play in the rink, without question. But like everything else it's gone too far. You have to get back to the basics of what was the reason that minor hockey exists today. The principal reason was to help kids, to give them something to do, keep their interest, improve their social and playing skills. Every now and then a player will come through the program and be like a Bobby Orr. There is no planning it, it just happens. Hockey is a wonderful game but there are lots of other sports out there. There is nothing wrong with going to a hockey camp in the summer but the athlete shouldn't feel he or she is obligated. I really think that playing other sports enhances the hockey if that is their number one sport."

Danny was the 12th player in the history of the game to score 50 goals at a time when it was extremely rare. In the 1980s everything opened up and there were lots of 50-goal scorers. Wayne Gretzky got 92.

"Players talk about the Toronto Maple Leafs of 1968 having five 20- goal scorers. That was your measuring stick. Keep it around that area. If you got 40 you didn't get a $50,000 raise. You might get $1,500 raise. There were years in Minnesota where I feel I could have scored a few more goals. I had 34 goals on two occasions. Under the circumstances I felt I could have scored 30 goals a year and not have to put much pressure on myself. Keep in mind that management would always expect more the next year. They were right. From 34 to 40 wasn't too far off. The problem was that you put yourself in a situation where the expectations of the management was that you were going to get 40 goals or more every year. If at Christmas you only had 14 or 15, then you would start to feel the pressure. I was called into the office numerous times, so it didn't take me long to catch on."

Danny also won the showdown competition 2 years in a row. The first showdown involved players from the NHL whereas the second one fea-

tured the best players in the world. The skills were skating, stick-han-
dling, passing and shooting. Danny said some of the players were on the
ice a lot in the summer. He wasn't too concerned because he said all he
had to do was shoot and score. Danny told me a little secret why he lost
the third one,

"The only reason Danny jokes that he lost the third one is that
Vladislav Tretiak brought in a little Russian vodka because it was
an International shoot-out. Everybody in the dressing room including Derryl Sittler, Guy Lafleur, the whole bunch of us had a toast to
hockey. Tretiak was the ring leader and opened up a big hockey
bag with little bottles of vodka. So we had a toast. It was a lot of
fun even though I didn't win. It is memories like these that you
can't buy."

Danny Grant was an iron man in hockey. He played 566 consecutive
games. In today's day and age that would amount to 7 full seasons of an
80 game schedule. Hockey is undoubtedly a fast-paced, hard-hitting game
and a punishing sport. Danny suffered several aches and bruises during the
streak. He played with a pulled muscle in his right shoulder that lasted
three weeks. He had a bad case of the flu one weekend and the Wings team
physician gave him a shot and he played the next night.

Danny loved the game and was dedicated to the game of hockey.
During the beginning of his streak in 1969, he was knocked totally unconscious in a game against "The Broadstreet Bullies" - The Philadelphia
Flyers. Bill Masterson died on the ice of a similar head injury the year
before. Danny remembers getting a stick in the mouth and being knocked
to the ice unconscious. When he came to he was taken to the hospital by
ambulance. This was on a Sunday evening. On the following Wednesday
with 8 stitches in his mouth and 10 more in his head, plus having a con-
cussion, he was back in the Wings' line-up wearing a helmet. He scored
the fifth and tying goal in the game. "The doctor said I would be groggy
for a few days and I was that night." He says about playing, "Sometimes
I felt I was ok and other times it was like walking in a dream. Today you
hear a lot about concussions but in those days it was just a regular occur-
rence. Everything was so misty and unreal."

Danny tried a comeback with the L.A. Kings in 77-79. His efforts were
in vain so he retired. Danny's final stats in the NHL were: Games played,
735, Goals 263, assists 273, for a total of 536 points.

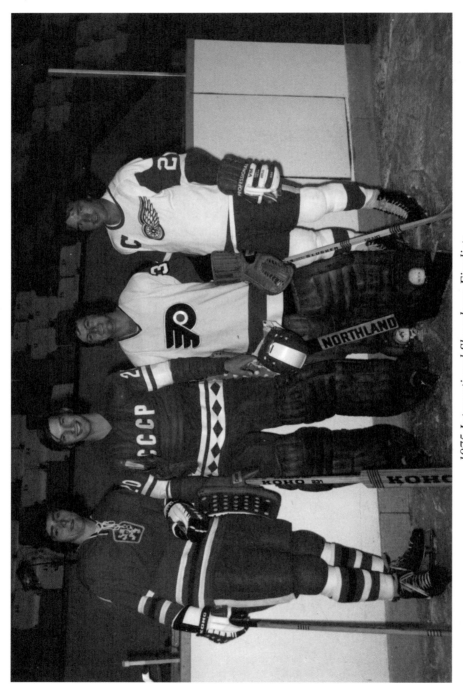

1975 International Showdown Finalists
Ivan Hlinka, Vladislav Tretiak, Wayne Stephenson, Danny Grant

Danny mentions some other New Brunswickers who toiled in the NHL in recent years: Willie O'Ree, Buster Harvey, Tony Currie, Rollie Melanson, Don Sweeney, Yvan Vautour, Charlie Bourgeois, Mike Eagles and Greg Malone.

When Danny retired he and the family moved back home to Fredericton. Life after pro hockey was a transition period which was made much easier by becoming involved with local hockey.

"Some of the most fun I had outside of playing was coaching Intermediate "A" hockey. I got a few calls from guys like Tim Gillies, Murray Shanks and Scott Walker asking me to coach. Finally I agreed. My only rules were that the 20 guys be committed and show up for practices and games. In my first year, 1979-80, we advanced to the Hardy Cup finals in Burnaby, B.C.. It was probably one of the most wonderful experiences I had in my life.

We started the team in 1979-80 called the Fredericton Capitals with a bunch of local kids that wanted to play hockey. Ten Frederictonians, including a few interested players, got together and put $50.00 into a pot in order to purchase the team. We were fortunate in acquiring Fred Curelier, who was an all star goalie with St. F.X. of the AUAA. He certainly captured the hearts of many fans in Fredericton. When Saint John Warriors folded we added Blair Nicholson and Ken MacLeod. We travelled all over N.B. and P.E.I. and eventually played for the Eastern Canadian Championship in Fredericton against Forbes Kennedy and the Charlottetown Islanders.. If you weren't at the rink at 4:30 p.m. for an 8 p.m. game you were out of luck. I believe the series will go down in the annals of hockey history as one of the greatest amateur sporting events ever witnessed at the York Arena and in the City of Fredericton. We won in 4 games."

After coaching the Capitals Danny put together a team called the Moosehead Golden Oldies. Some of the players on the team were Buster Harvey, Red Ouellette, Bob Warner, Errol Thompson, and Bill Riley. The team played in small communities all over N.B. and P.E.I. playing against local teams and raising money for minor hockey programs.

Just when Danny thought he was finally out of hockey for good, he got a call from Gilles Leger, director of Player Personnel for the Quebec Nordiques in 1981. The Nordiques wanted to put a farm team in

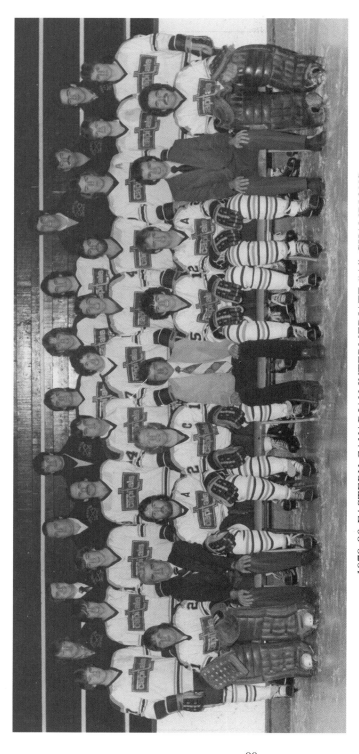

1979-80 EASTERN CANADIAN INTERMEDIATE "A" CHAMPIONS

Front row: Don MacTavish, Murray Shanks (President), Dave Neill, Alfie Hamill, Danny Grant, Mike MacKay, Larry Mayhew, Tim Gillies (G.M.), Fred Cuvelier

2nd row: Bob McSorley, Mike Barry, Wayne Hallihan, Dick Yeomans, Bob Martin, Tony Grant, Mark Rickard, Bob Bell, Blair Nicholson, Charlie Bird, J.J. McInnis

3rd row: Gerry Endall, Jim Chessie (P.R.), John Balmain (50/50 draw), Bob Lamb (PR), Ken MacLeod, Keith Allaby, Blaine Phillips, Scott Walker (Trainer), Charlie O'Leary (Equipment Mgr.), Marshall Goodwin (Equipment Mgr.)

Missing from photo: Marcus Hodgson, John Benson and Donnie Gallant

Fredericton and the team would be coached by Jacques Demers, who went on to have a distinguished career in the NHL. Danny became President and the rest is history.

Danny was once again out of hockey or so he thought. One evening two young gentlemen showed up at his doorstep, Shane Feeney and Robbie Boldon from the local Midget AAA program informing Danny their coach had quit and asked if he would consider the job just for the rest of the year. Nine years later he was still there.

During these years the Fredericton Boldon Red Wings, later the Fredericton Canadiens, won five Atlantic Championships and went to the nationals four times. The program raised the bar for Midget AAA hockey in Atlantic Canada. Gary and Carol McKinley were the managers and Kevin Pottle and Danny were behind the bench.

After coaching the Intermediate team Danny thought that nothing would be as exciting as the series with Charlottetown. He found coaching the Midgets to be both exciting and challenging. He says the main reasons the program was successful was the team had the full support of parents and players. Danny reminisces:

> "I can still see Johnny Gee speeding through centre ice, Brad Shepherd dishing out punishing checks, Todd Sparks snapping in a wrist shot from the top of the circle, Shane Kenny's blast from the point, my son Jeff patrolling left wing, Peter Clark getting hit in Thunder Bay and going to the other team's bench. I also remember the great times we had with parents, Dr. Mike and Dorothy Johnson, Marty and Fran Wilson, Richard and Margie Clark, Gordie and Millie Boldon to name a few and of course, Wayne Naugle, our trainer who passed away a few years ago."

Next thing for Danny was a call from Mike Johnston, who was the coach of the UNB hockey team. He was leaving to go with the Canadian Olympic team. Mike asked if he would take over the team for one year. He agreed, not knowing that he would be there for two years from 1995-1997. Then Mike Kelly was hired on a full-time basis in 1996-97 and taught courses as well. Danny stayed on as assistant. The team went to the Nationals but lost. The following year Mike Kelly's team won the National Championship and Danny's recruitments helped no doubt. In 1997-98 Danny was the head coach of the Halifax Mooseheads. The following year, 1998-99, Danny was in charge of the player personnel.

Danny gives a lot of the credit for his success to his hometown and to his parents:

"I have and always will be a proud New Brunswicker. There is a little community in the heart of New Brunswick called Barkers Point that I will always remember for being the greatest place in the world to be a kid.

My mom is a 'sweetheart'. She was one of the prettiest girls in New Brunswick when she married Dad and is still very beautiful. She never said a bad word about anybody and has tremendous faith in people. She enjoys the simple things in life. She often says that people today are losing sight of what is really important. I agree 100 per cent.

I have not said anything about my father whom I respect more than any man on earth. He was and still is my real hero. He worked hard all his life. He gave our family everything he could and was a genuine role model to look up to.

Besides my parents, who have supported me throughout my career, there is one person that has been there for me for over 34 years and that has been my wife Linda. We have shared some wonderful times and we shared some tough times. She put up with the highs and lows that go along with a professional athlete's career.

She knew how to cheer me up when things were not going well and she also knew when to rein me in when I started getting carried away with my own success. She gave me two wonderful children, Kelly and Jeff, and kept our family together while I was travelling all over the country doing what I loved, playing hockey. I loved her from the day we met and I still love her the same way today. She has always been my real strength."

Today, October 2002, Danny is working for Enbridge Gas New Brunswick in sales and marketing. He is also an assistant coach of the St. Thomas hockey team.

When Danny Grant broke the modern record of 30 goals set by a rookie in the NHL by Boom Boom Geoffrion at the Montreal Canadiens, the Premier of New Brunswick, Louis Robichaud, sent a telegram.

It read: "All New Brunswick is proud of your record breaking performance, which shows your outstanding capabilities and shows what New Brunswickers can do. I know all people in the province join with me in wishing you continued success."

Ernie Fitzsimmons is a hockey historian and president of the Society for International Hockey Research.

"Danny Grant ranks right there with Al MacInnis, Gordie Drillon and one or two others as the best player ever to come out of the Maritimes," Fitzsimmons said. "He didn't just play, he played very well and had one of the best shots in the NHL."

Mike Eagles, an NHL veteran of 17 seasons of professional hockey, says about Danny scoring 50 goals,

"It goes to show how good Danny Grant was at that time. He was one of the most elite players to ever play in the NHL."

He says in regards to Danny's Iron Man feat,

"I can't imagine anybody ever doing it. I know from actual experience that hockey is a very punishing sport. You are seldom 100 per cent and often play banged up and bruised. To me personally, it is a testament to the true character of Danny Grant."

Sports writer Joe Falls for the Detroit Free Press wrote about Danny on April 14, 1975:

"Grant is different in that he gets his job done and gets it done without a flourish. You don't hear Danny Grant popping off. You don't hear him griping and groaning. You don't hear anything about him. All you see is the red light going on ... again ... and again ... and again.

He is a throwback to the days when athletes seemed to play for the sheer pleasure of playing. In fact, he performs like one of the oldtimers, working his wing with perseverance and preferring the wrist shot to the celebrated slapshot."